Walt

Resa

Text by Jennie Hess
Updated by Jason Mitchell
Edited by Roger Williams
Cover photograph © Disney Enterprises, Inc.
Layout Concept: Klaus Geisler
Picture Editor: Hilary Genin
Managing Editor: Tony Halliday

Berlitz® POCKET GUIDE

Walt Disney World® Resort & Orlando

Thirteenth Edition (2003)
Updated 2006

PHOTOGRAPHY
©Busch Entertainment Corporation 84, 85; Corbis 15, 17; ©Disney Enterprises, Inc. 6, 22, 25, 29, 31, 33, 35, 45, 49, 52, 55, 56, 59, 86; Annabel Elston 46; Martin Gostelow 41, 81; Ronald Grant Archive 51; Library of Congress 18, 21; ©Orlando/Orange County CVB 12, 20, 77, 83, 89, 90, 92; Mark Read 26, 78; ©2002 SeaWorld Orlando 11, 2, 60, 71, 74; Science Photo Library 37, 39; ©2002 Universal Orlando title, 8, 10, 63, 65, 66, 67, 68, 69, 70, 94, 96, 99, 100; Wet'n'Wild 75, 76

CONTACTING THE EDITORS
Every effort has been made to provide accurate information in this publication, but changes are inevitable. The publisher cannot be responsible for any resulting loss, inconvenience or injury. We would appreciate it if readers would call our attention to any errors or outdated information by contacting Berlitz Publishing, PO Box 7910, London SE1 1WE, England. Fax: (44) 20 7403 0290;
e-mail: berlitz@apaguide.co.uk
www.berlitzpublishing.com

© 2006 Apa Publications GmbH & Co. Verlag KG, Singapore Branch, Singapore

Printed in Singapore by Insight Print Services (Pte) Ltd, 38 Joo Koon Road, Singapore 628990. Tel: (65) 6865-1600. Fax: (65) 6861-6438

Berlitz Trademark Reg. U.S. Patent Office and other countries. Marca Registrada

This book makes reference to various Disney copyrighted characters, trademarks, marks and registered marks owned by The Walt Disney Company and Disney Enterprises, Inc.

➤ Tomorrowland, Disney's futuristic world where Jules Verne meets Buzz Lightyear (page 33)

Sharks patroling at Disney's Living Seas, which has the largest salt water fish tank in the world (page 43) ▲

Gatorland in Kissimmee where 5,000 gaters live (page 79) ➤

Big Thunder Mountain Railroad is a rocky highlight of Disney's Magic Kingdom Park (page 29) ▼

TOP TEN ATTRACTIONS

Visit the Kennedy Space Center on the Florida coast (page 82)

Go on safari and have some close encounters at Disney's Animal Kingdom (page 54)

The Chinese pavilion at Disney's World Showcase Lagoon where the sights of the whole world come to Disney's door (page 44)

Cinderella Castle in Disney's Fantasyland, where fairytales come to life (page 30)

Wet 'n' Wild is the place for a soaking (page 75)

Learn how it's done at Magic of Disney Animation (page 52)

CONTENTS

INTRODUCTION

The Magic Kingdom opened its gates to the public near the sleepy central Florida city of Orlando on Friday, 1 October 1971. The date was chosen to avoid large summer crowds and traffic snarls. Even so, 10,000 visitors came. By Thanksgiving in late November, the figure had risen to 60,000 and the park was full. Since then, the Walt Disney World Resort has exploded into a wonderland of attractions laying claim as the busiest vacation center on Earth.

Until the park arrived, Orlando was known as a center for citrus-fruit farming and relied on its lakes and crocodile farms to attract curious visitors. The climate was a major factor, making it an ideal choice for a year-round theme park. Today access is easy on the Interstate and the airport is linked to America's cities as well as to cities around the world. Peak times for visiting are Christmas and early January, the weeks before and during Easter, June to late August, and long holiday weekends in the United States, such as Thanksgiving. Winter in central Florida is generally delightful. It's hot and humid in the summer, but you can cool off in hotel pools and water parks and spend more time outdoors in the evenings. There is really no bad time to visit.

The Disney property covers an area of 48 sq miles (124 sq km) or 30,500 acres (12,342 hectares), almost the size of San Francisco. It has a staff, or cast, of about 50,000, and on any day around 100,000 visitors enjoy the attractions.

Situated some 25 miles (40km) southwest of the city of Orlando and nearer the once-sleepy cattle town of Kissimmee, the home of Mickey Mouse and friends began with the Magic Kingdom Park and a cluster of Disney hotels. It grew quickly to include Epcot – inspired by the World's fair – Disney-MGM Studios, water parks, more hotels, nightclubs, a sports complex, good restaurants, and Disney's Animal Kingdom, which became by far the largest of Disney's world-wide theme parks.

Added Attractions

As Disney grew, so did the attractions around it. SeaWorld Orlando, which opened two years after the Magic Kingdom, has held its own in the competition for visitors by doing what it does best – entertaining and informing visitors about marine life – and by building its own exhilarating rides to attract thrill seekers.

Universal Studios Florida opened in 1990 and added a new edge to the theme-park mix, giving travelers a movie-themed choice apart from the Disney fortress. Just before the new millennium, Universal threw a quick one-two in the battle of the parks by opening the Islands of Adventure thrill

Movie-set ready for action at Universal Studios

park and CityWalk entertainment complex. This empire is collectively called Universal Orlando Resort.

> **Walt Disney World Resort has only ever closed once – when Hurricane Andrew threatened in 1992.**

Theme parks aren't the only reason to visit this sun-drenched city of fun and fantasy. The area's natural wonders, including hundreds of lakes and canals, set the scene for unlimited recreational activity from canoeing and bass fishing to hiking, biking, hot-air ballooning, and parasailing.

Orlando, Disney, and the surrounding area collectively have around 100,000 hotel rooms – second only to Las Vegas for accommodations in a US metropolitan area. Many visitors fly directly into Orlando International Airport, a bright, sleek airport that has grown rapidly to become one of the busiest in the world. Britons top the list of foreign visitors: more than a million fly to Orlando each year, enough to fill 10 jumbo jets every day. Other travelers arrive in Miami, 220 miles (353km) to the south, connected by good roads and frequent flights to Orlando. Countless visitors drive from all over North America, and train and bus services link Orlando with the rest of Florida and major US cities.

Walt Disney himself once predicted that his original park, Disneyland, California, would never be finished, but he wasn't expecting slow progress. He meant that it would constantly evolve and expand. Likewise, Walt Disney World Resort continues to grow; though Epcot, Disney-MGM Studios and Disney's Animal Kingdom are complete, they are constantly changing.

Resorts and Hotels

Initially, there were three Disney hotels. Today, there are a score of Disney-owned resorts and several hotels on Disney property which are run by major hotel entities. In all, there are more than 25,000 rooms and over 700 campsites within the complex.

Walt Disney World Resort's ace in the pocket is its status as a complete resort destination offering much more than a day in the theme parks. There are enough attractions to keep travelers happy, whether they're families, seniors, singles, or honeymooners. In fact, Walt Disney World Resort has become one of the most popular honeymoon destinations in the world. The majority of its visitors are adults – for them Walt Disney World Resort operates a colorful mix of bars, nightclubs, first-rate restaurants, and theatrical entertainment such as Cirque du Soleil. With pools and sandy beaches (yes, this far from the sea), lakes and water sports, tennis courts, and more golf facilities than any Florida golf resort, you might stay within the Disney 'borders' for your entire trip. But you shouldn't. There are too many other top-notch attractions in the Orlando area.

Hard Rock Hotel at Universal

Universal

Universal Studios Florida opened in 1990 with its own production studios and a fresh new venue for guests to play among movie-themed sets, rides, and attractions. With game shows, films, and other TV production taking hold, the area has begun to gain a reputation as

'Hollywood East.' Located on a 444-acre (180-hectare) site north of International Drive, Universal Studios is close to the key I-4 highway. After nine years of luring millions of visitors, Universal opened Islands of Adventure, promising a theme park visit on the wild side with monster roller-coasters and other thrill-a-minute attractions. CityWalk, with

SeaWorld Orlando

celebrity restaurants, nightclubs and plenty of live entertainment, rounds out the Universal Orlando Resort.

Busch Entertainment and SeaWorld

SeaWorld Orlando came to Florida in 1973 as an up-to-date version of the marine parks that have been a Florida tradition since the 1920s. Today, it offers more than its popular performing whales and dolphins, clowning sea lions, and parading penguins. Busch Entertainment Corporation, part of the giant brewing empire Anheuser-Busch, bought SeaWorld in 1989, adding it to their existing properties – Busch Gardens in Tampa and Cypress Gardens south of Orlando. They have multiplied attractions and added to the variety, making SeaWorld Orlando a logical stop on any trip to central Florida.

Orlando

After you've spent a few days in the theme parks and seen the impressively gaudy strip called International Drive, you may wonder whether Orlando does have a city center. The answer is yes, although the millions who go straight from the airport to Walt Disney World Resort or Kissimmee never see it. From the top of Disney's highest building, it's a speck on the horizon. Even International Drive, halfway between, is 9 miles (15km) from downtown Orlando.

Until the 1960s, Orlando was an old-fashioned inland town dotted with lakes and swamps. True, it had several charming suburbs built by prosperous migrants who were retreating from northern winters, and it still has them. But all else has changed beyond recognition. Today, several large companies have headquarters here, and many sports stars have made Orlando their home.

Good roads put all the attractions nearby within easy reach. Less than an hour's drive east is the Atlantic Coast and Kennedy Space Center, with the Gulf Coast not much farther to the west. There's more than enough to enjoy during a stay of a week or two. No wonder people keep coming back.

The Kennedy Space Center at Cape Canaveral is a big local draw

A BRIEF HISTORY

Walter Elias Disney was born on 5 December 1901 in Chicago. His father was a building contractor of Anglo-Irish stock and Canadian birth. When Walt was still a toddler, the family moved to a farm in Marceline, Missouri. All the children, even the youngest, had to help on the farm. Walt showed an interest in drawing from an early age and took his first art lessons in Kansas City when he was 14. In 1919 he served as an ambulance driver with the US Army in France, too late to witness action in World War I. As surviving photographs show, he continued to draw during this time, though evidence of his talents is confined to caricatures on his ambulance and fake medals on buddies' jackets.

Walt had seen the simple animated films of the time and was sure he could do better. In Kansas City he teamed up with artist Ubbe 'Ub' Iwerks to make commercials and animated versions of *Cinderella* and *Little Red Riding Hood*.

Disney Goes to Hollywood

In 1923, Disney packed his bags and moved to Los Angeles determined to make animated films that were more than just crude fillers. He wanted to create characters who had a life of their own and emotions that people could recognize and relate to. He formed a partnership with his older brother Roy, who was already in California, to produce a series of shorts called *The Alice Comedies* (for which *Alice's Wonderland* was the pilot), combining live action and animation, a formula Disney returned to years later with *Mary Poppins*. Iwerks joined him to look after the artwork and Roy Disney ran the business side.

The pattern was soon set. Disney had the ideas and, as he explained, 'pollinated' the various departments, like a bee

> By 1926, Disney had stopped drawing. Later, he was embarrassed when children assumed he had created his films himself – yet he couldn't draw them a sketch of Pluto or Goofy.

moving from flower to flower. Oswald the Lucky Rabbit brought recognition, but Disney lost the rights to the character in a contractual dispute with a New York distributor. From then on he retained absolute control of his company's creations, defending them fiercely with copyrights and trademarks, a practice that continues to this day.

The Birth of Mickey Mouse

According to his own account, Disney was on a train back from New York when he came up with the idea of a new hero, a mouse to be called... Mortimer! When he told his wife, Lillian, she wisely suggested the name Mickey instead. Ub Iwerks drew the soon-to-be-famous character to Walt's satisfaction, with the famous circular ears, velvet trousers, big round-toed shoes, and four-finger gloves.

It was 1928, and Mickey Mouse appeared in the silent film *Plane Crazy*, which came out at the same time as the first talking picture, *The Jazz Singer*. Sensing the way the film business was moving, Disney withdrew his film, and re-released it with a soundtrack. In 1928, Mickey starred in the first animated film with synchronized sound, *Steamboat Willie*. Walt himself provided Mickey's falsetto voice, and continued to do so for many years. Minnie Mouse appeared in the same film, when Mickey hauled her on board with a boathook. *Steamboat Willie* was a huge success. In some countries the characters were renamed (in Italy Mickey was called Topolino, the name given to Fiat's popular car).

Disney's dream had come true. The sheer quality of the work, the attention to detail, the wit and talent of the artists, and his own perfectionism had lifted animated films to new heights. He had the respect of filmmakers, who watched Disney productions for new ideas. And the public loved the characters. In 1934, Donald Duck's arrival brought a personality to counteract Mickey's essential cheerfulness. The irascible duck in the silly sailor suit whose pride always led to a fall became an even bigger favorite than Mickey.

Disney was a pioneer in the use of color, with the *Silly Symphony* series starting in 1929, which included *Flowers and Trees* (1933). The stories were set in the fairy-tale landscapes that sprang to life in the theme parks many years later.

Walt Disney was now ready to climb the ultimate mountain – the first full-length animated feature film, *Snow White and the Seven Dwarfs*. To attain the quality he had in mind, fine artwork was needed. The 83-minute film didn't use just 10 times the drawings and painted 'cels' as an eight-minute

Walt and Roy Disney announce plans for a new theme park

film. Far more were needed to give the human characters the smooth movements of live actors. He hired 300 artists, bringing the total to 750, and took more than three years.

Finally, in late 1937, *Snow White and the Seven Dwarfs* was given a star-studded premiere in Hollywood, the first ever for an animated production. That first audience was enchanted by the film, which won a special Academy Award: a big Oscar for Snow White and seven little ones for the Dwarfs. Pinocchio, an even more intricate achievement, followed three years later.

Disney broke new ground again in 1940 with *Fantasia*, setting beautiful, funny, and bizarre scenes to the music of Bach, Beethoven, Stravinsky, and Tchaikovsky, and Mickey Mouse played The Sorcerer's Apprentice, whose delusions of omnipotence unleash forces beyond his control. It was almost a metaphor for the war that had begun in Europe and was about to enmesh the United States. When it did, Disney Studios made training films, with GIs adopting as a mascot the suitably aggressive Donald Duck in commando uniform.

Building the Dream

After World War II, Disney made *Song of the South*, combining live action and animation. This was followed by a number of all-live films including *Treasure Island*, *Swiss Family Robinson*, and *20,000 Leagues Under the Sea*, which generated ideas for future theme-park attractions. The animated features in the 1950s – *Cinderella*, *Alice in Wonderland*, *Peter Pan* and *Sleeping Beauty* – also served as inspiration.

Disney had always loved the idea of amusement parks, but when he visited them with his daughters, they seemed tawdry and unimaginative. The idea for a theme park of his own came in 1947 when, on doctors' orders, he was supposed to be relaxing, but for him that meant throwing him-

Disney with Shirley Temple and the Seven Dwarf Oscars

self into a new project, this time a model railway. As it grew bigger and bigger, his dream of a park where parents and children could have fun together took hold. He presented the plan to his brother Roy, who wouldn't agree to invest more than $10,000 in the 'screwy idea.' As Walt Disney's story goes, he raised the capital himself, on his life insurance policy.

The First Park

By 1952 he had set up a company called WED (his initials) and sketched out the plans. He acquired 160 acres (65 hectares) of land in Anaheim, on the southern edge of Los Angeles, where he built not only a railway, but a complete 'Disneyland' populated with his vast array of characters. His designers created a huge stage set, on which visitors moved from scene to scene like stars of the show. It was more than a fairground or an amusement park. There had never been anything like it. Disneyland Park opened on 17 July 1955, and was an overwhelming success, with more than 4 million visitors in the first year, rising to 10 million a year as its fame spread. The number of attractions doubled, while executives learned how to handle such unprecedented numbers.

But Walt Disney was not entirely happy. Fast-food and souvenir shops had spread to the borders of Disneyland, creaming off revenues that he felt should belong to Walt Disney Productions.

A New World in Florida

Disney was determined not to make the same mistake twice.

Aligator farms were the first local tourist attraction

As he began searching for a suitable theme park site in the eastern United States, one prerequisite was a great deal of real estate. The others were a year-round sunny climate and good travel connections that could expand to handle the traffic. His scouts found what he was looking for in central Florida, near the quiet town of Orlando. Nominees started to buy up land, picking up 27,500 acres (11,000 hectares) by 1964 at the cost of $6 million. If word had leaked that Walt Disney was behind it, prices would have skyrocketed. When locals did eventually catch on, costs multiplied a hundredfold overnight.

The Animated Films

1930s *Snow White and the Seven Dwarfs* (1937)

1940s *Pinocchio* (1940), *Fantasia* (1940), *Dumbo* (1941), *Bambi* (1942), *Saludos Amigos* (1943), *The Three Caballeros* (1945), *Make Mine Music* (1946), *Fun and Fancy Free* (1947), *Melody Time* (1948), *The Adventures of Ichabod and Mr. Toad* (1949)

1950s *Cinderella* (1950), *Alice in Wonderland* (1951), *Peter Pan* (1953), *Lady and the Tramp* (1955), *Sleeping Beauty* (1959)

1960s *One Hundred and One Dalmatians* (1961), *The Sword in the Stone* (1963), *The Jungle Book* (1967)

1970s *The Aristocats* (1970), *Robin Hood* (1973), *The Many Adventures of Winnie the Pooh* (1977), *The Rescuers* (1977)

1980s *The Fox and the Hound* (1981), *The Black Cauldron* (1985), *The Great Mouse Detective* (1986), *Oliver & Company* (1988), *The Little Mermaid* (1989)

1990s *The Rescuers Down Under* (1990), *Beauty and the Beast* (1991), *Aladdin* (1992), *The Lion King* (1994), *Pocahontas* (1995), *The Hunchback of Notre Dame* (1996), *Hercules* (1997), *Mulan* (1998), *Tarzan* (1999)

2000s *Fantasia* (2000), *Monsters, Inc.* (2001), *Lilo and Stitch* (2002), *Treasure Planet* (2002), Chicken Little (2005)

Disney planned a park along similar lines of the original Disneyland, except larger. But his dream went much farther than size. He envisaged nothing less than a 'living, breathing city of the future,' his 'Experimental Prototype Community of Tomorrow,' known as Epcot. He outlined his plan in a film but it was the last film he would make. In December 1966, he died quite suddenly, of complications following surgery for lung cancer.

Roy O. Disney had not always seen eye-to-eye with his brother, but they had recently set aside their differences, and Roy became chairman of Walt Disney Productions. At his

> **Walt Disney World Resort is in a 'state' of its own, administering its own planning, with the power to build roads and water systems and run its own police and fire-fighting forces.**

suggestion, the Florida project was given the name Walt Disney World – a generous tribute to his brother. ('Resort' was added later in an attempt to emphasize the range of activities.)

Preparation began in 1967 and construction followed in 1969. By October 1971, the Magic Kingdom was open. This time, guests could stay in Disney hotels, swim, play golf and tennis, dine, and be entertained without leaving Disney territory. When everyone from top executives to the newest cast member had to help park cars or cook hot-dogs, it began a tradition – cross-utilization, or 'Cross-U' in Disney parlance – that continues during busy holiday periods.

Entertainment Comes First

Epcot opened in 1982, resembling a World's Fair. Future World recalls the celebration of technology Disney had proposed, while World Showcase comprised pavilions of several nations with replicas of their famous buildings. Both are true to Walt Disney's dictum: 'I would rather entertain and hope that people learn, than educate and hope they're entertained.'

Tokyo Disneyland Resort followed in 1983 and was another hit. Soon the parks became financially more important than film-making. Believing that Epcot's costs and the shortage of new film successes had weakened Walt Disney Productions, outside interests planned a take-over.

Perhaps it was just lucky, but the 50th birthday of gutsy little Donald Duck in 1984 coincided with the beginning of a new era – and the company's survival and rejuvenation.

Back on Top

As the dust settled, Michael Eisner became the chairman and chief executive. The family connection continued when Roy E. Disney, son of Roy O., became head of animation. The Disney organization was transformed with a string of film successes, television series, and fresh contracts for Disney products. One of Eisner's first acts was to sign an agreement with the French government to build the Euro Disney Resort (now known as Disneyland Paris Resort) east of Paris, which opened in April 1992.

The attractions of Walt Disney World Resort were increased in 1989 with Typhoon Lagoon water park, Pleasure Island entertainment complex, and Disney-MGM Studios, where visitors could see real film sets and TV studios. An East Coast animation department was opened, which collaborated with the West Coast team to make *Beauty and the Beast* and *Aladdin*. *Mulan* was the first full-length feature to be produced entirely at Disney-MGM Studios.

Walt Disney the visionary

The fourth Florida theme park, Disney's $800-million Animal Kingdom, a 'live-animal adventure park' in a 500-acre (202-hectare) site, opened in April 1998, while half a hemisphere away in Asia, Disney Hong Kong opened its gates in 2005.

WHERE TO GO

Covering 43 sq miles (111 sq km) and with an average daily visitor population of 100,000, **Walt Disney World® Resort** is by far the largest of Orlando's theme parks. The resort lies off Interstate 4, 16 miles (26km) from downtown Orlando. Halfway between Disney and the town is **Universal Studios Orlando** and between Disney and Universal lies the aquarium and theme park of **SeaWorld**.

GETTING AROUND

Most visitors who come decide before leaving home which of the theme parks they will visit, and many will not stray from the theme park of their choice. But it is possible to visit more than one, and it is certainly possible to come back for more, so these pages should help you to choose your ideal destination. There are many inclusive deals for visitors, and you should shop around before you leave home.

Faced with so many attractions, you will need a plan of action, especially if this is your first visit or your time is limited. How do you decide what to do and the order in which to do it? We don't suggest sticking to a rigid schedule, but unless you allocate your time wisely, you'll find it difficult to take full advantage of all that's offered. Your first step is to abandon any idea of 'seeing everything.' Select the parks you want to visit and then the most appealing rides and attractions within them.

WALT DISNEY WORLD RESORT

You can buy one-day, one-park tickets, although such a short visit isn't recommended. If you do have only one day, however, select one park and spend the entire day there. For longer visits, the Walt Disney World Resort sells money-saving passes for four days (all theme parks) and five days (all theme parks as well as other attractions). Passes don't have to be used on consecutive days.

If you're staying at one of the resorts on the monorail system, that is the quickest way to reach some of the attractions. If you're staying elsewhere on Disney property, use the free Walt Disney World Resort buses. If you drive yourself, you'll be directed to vast parking lots. Guests at a Disney property have free parking if they show their hotel ID card. Note where you leave your car – rows are numbered but the spaces are not, and areas are named. If you think you may forget whether you're in Grumpy, Sleepy, or Dopey, write down the details.

The Magic Kingdom Park

From the main Magic Kingdom parking lot, trams whisk you to the ticket area, where you can take a ferryboat or a monorail train to the park gates. Beyond the tracks and railway station of Walt Disney World Resort, the scene opens out into **Town Square**, an idealized version of a small American town from the year 1900 with buildings at four-fifths real size, a trick called 'forced perspective'. The Magic Kingdom Park is the heart and soul of the Resort, a gentle place for children and families, that is constantly updated, but essentially little changed from its original idea.

Throughout the day Town Square buzzes with band performances, parades, and flag ceremonies.

You can board a horse-drawn trolley, horseless carriage, or double-decker bus to **Cinderella Castle** *(see page 30)*; or a fire engine

Attraction opening times vary, from around 9am to 8pm daily. Entrance fees are between $20 and $60 with discounts for under-10s. Children under three go free.

will drive you down Main Street; or you might prefer the stroll, checking out shops and a few attractions from bygone days. On the right, there are interactive kiosks featuring historic footage of Walt Disney and his creations. Labeled 'Discover the Stories Behind the Magic,' they lie behind the Town Square exposition hall.

Across the street and down an alley, you can get an old-fashioned shave or a haircut at **Harmony Barber Shop**, often featuring a barbershop quartet.

The circular plaza, ringed by water, is the hub of the Magic Kingdom, with bridges and walkways leading to different lands like spokes of a wheel. Check 'tip boards' on Main Street and in other lands for the wait times at the most popular rides.

To begin this adventure, we choose to go clockwise, starting with a sharp left turn at the plaza to Adventureland.

Main Street, U.S.A.

Adventureland

Adventureland consists of some classic Disney attractions. The huge **Swiss Family Treehouse** is built among the branches of a faux Banyan that's almost a one-tree forest. The tree is concrete, and the leaves are synthetic. You climb winding stairways through the home of the famous ship-wrecked Robinson family. (The classic 1812 novel *The Swiss Family Robinson* by Johann David Wyss was the subject of a live-action Disney film with John Mills and Dorothy McGuire.)

In **Jungle Cruise**, the vegetation is real, and mechanical lions, giraffes, hippos, and bathing elephants look pretty convincing. Geography goes haywire as you travel through jungles and rain-forests and past a Cambodian temple. Across the way, **The Enchanted Tiki Room – Under New Management** combines Disney's first-ever Audio-Animatronics® birds with stars from *The Lion King* and *Aladdin*. Perennially popular, the **Pirates of the Caribbean** sets up all kinds of skulldug-gery in a raid on an island fort, as your ship sails through the Spanish Main with rum-swilling bucca-neers and lots of yo-ho-ho spirit. Smaller children may be frightened by some of the scenes.

Magic Kingdom visitor

On Your Marks...

If you've ever seen the start of the London or Boston marathons, you'll have an idea of what 'rope-drop' is like. At the end of Main Street, U.S.A., the early birds assemble during the hour between the main gate opening and the official opening, held back from their goals by a simple rope across the road. Nobody pushes. What is it about Walt Disney World Resort that makes everyone so well behaved?

At 9am sharp, the two cast members in charge open a gap in the middle and move the rope aside. A wedge of assorted humanity, led by the most agile, heads through like a flying arrow, before splitting into left, center, and right-hand streams. The leftists are making for Frontierland. The center party goes for the passage through Cinderella Castle on the way to the attractions of Fantasyland and the charge of the right brigade is bound for Tomorrowland and Space Mountain.

Frontierland

The frontier in Frontierland is that of the 19th-century American Wild West, when pioneers panned for gold or drove their cattle across the range. The cast dresses for the part in kerchiefs and denim, bonnets and gingham, while the architecture runs the gamut from log cabin to fancy façade.

Popular with teenagers is the explosive **Frontierland Shootin' Arcade**, where there are neither bullets nor pellets, but infrared beams fired by converted hunting rifles. Hits on the moving, pop-up and stationary targets trigger hilarious effects, including screaming ricochets and howlin' coyotes. There's a 50-cent charge for each round of 25 shots.

An ideal attraction for younger kids on the same street is **Country Bear Jamboree**, a crowd-pleaser for almost three decades in which Audio-Animatronics characters perform a humorous 17-minute stage show with country music and big bear antics.

Make the Most of Your Time

1. Meet with your family and choose preferred rides and attractions for each park. Look at the (free) park maps to work out a route.
2. Buy tickets (or four- or five-day passes) in advance at Walt Disney World Resort hotels or through travel agents.
3. Arrive early at the entrance, before the gates open *(see page 27)*, to beat the crowds and get the most from your ticket.
4. Consult entertainment schedules for parade and performance times.
5. Have lunch early, or late, to avoid the midday rush.
6. Leave all the shopping until after you've had your fill of attractions.
7. Visit indoor and sit-down shows in the early afternoon – for the shade and air-conditioning.
8. Leave time for relaxation, especially if you have small children. You may want to take a siesta at your hotel (remember to get your hand stamped to allow you to re-enter the parks).

High spots

Two of the highest hills in Florida are found here in the Magic Kingdom, where once there was citrus land and swamp. **Splash Mountain** is a log flume ride, where boats slowly climb the watery slopes, winding up anticipation. Scenes along the way come from *Song of the South*, the 1946 movie featuring the characters Brer Rabbit and Brer Fox. You pass through tunnels, twists, and turns before emerging over five stories up, where you'll hang in space for a breath-taking moment before racing headlong down the 45-degree slope (which almost feels like a vertical drop) into the briar-fringed pool below.

It is enough to elicit screams without inducing real terror, but you'll definitely get wet, so make sure you cover your cameras. Take note of boarding restrictions – nobody who suffers from back or neck problems should take the ride.

Although it's more funny than frightening, the same

restrictions apply on **Big Thunder Mountain Railroad**, a
roller coaster in an elaborate red-rock setting. Here, there are
no drops as steep as those on Splash Mountain, and many
young children enjoy the thrills without fear. Mining equipment from days gone by litters the hillside and Audio-Animatronics animals populate the slopes. You climb on board a
'runaway' mine train that chugs to the top of the hill before
rushing at breakneck speed around several bends, then up,
down, and all around the mountain.

You reach **Tom Sawyer Island** by raft. In complete contrast to the rest of the Magic Kingdom, more adventurous
children can run around here on their own, firing the guns of
Fort Langhorne, crossing swaying bridges and exploring
the caves and secret passages. This can be quite a time-
consuming expedition and is best kept for a second visit.
The island closes at dusk.

Big Thunder Mountain Railroad

© DISNEY ENTERPRISES, INC.

Liberty Square

Just across from the wooden shacks of the Wild West, you'll have spotted a more elegant building of the Colonial era, reminiscent of those around Philadelphia's Independence Hall. **The Hall of Presidents** brings to life every American president. Following a 25-minute big-screen, upbeat history of the US Constitution (best seats are at the back), each president takes a bow on stage. Notice how the presidents fidget during the presentation and the detail in their costumes, each painstakingly researched and recreated in period style.

➤ You can beat the heat *and* give yourself a real fright in **The Haunted Mansion**, where (count them if you can) 999 grim-grinning ghosts emerge from the dark. It's all good-humored, but still not for the very small or nervous. Surprisingly, the technology is several decades old – done with scrims, black light, mirrors, and projection.

Fantasyland

Walt Disney's dream was to make fairy tales come to life, and **Fantasyland** really embodies that spirit.

➤ Don't expect any thrilling rides inside **Cinderella Castle**, but spare a moment to inspect the fine mosaics that depict scenes from the famous 1950 Disney film. Even if you don't eat here, walk up the ceremonial staircase to Cinderella's Royal Table.

Several times a day, an energetic musical show hits the **Castle Forecourt Stage**. Many of the songs are Disney hits, and Disney characters join in with the dancing.

The Castle Forecourt also makes one of the most picturesque places for children to meet their favorite characters. Mickey, Minnie, Snow White, and their friends appear here several times a day under the shadow of the magical castle. Check for exact show times. Through the castle archway and straight ahead, the most traditional ride in the entire Kingdom, **Cinderella's Golden Carrousel**, is a merry-go-round of exquisite galloping horses.

Next door, you'll find **Dumbo the Flying Elephant**, where replicas circle and soar as riders control the height. Dumbo's manager, Timothy Mouse, 'directs' operations from atop the ride's hot-air balloon center. Dumbo is a hit with the very young, and it's best to ride during parade times when the line shortens.

Peter Pan's Flight, inspired by J. M. Barrie's book and the Disney movie of 1953, sends you flying through the 'night' in a miniature pirate ship, where you can meet Peter, Wendy, and scheming Captain Hook.

Cinderella Castle

➤ The charming **It's a Small World** is billed as 'the happiest cruise that ever sailed.' You can't help but smile at the hundreds of singing, dancing dolls dressed in folk costumes from every corner of the globe. The ride is busy but moves quickly.

Snow White and the Seven Dwarfs was Disney's first full-length animated feature film, and when it was released in 1937 some of it was considered to be too frightening for small children to watch. The same might be true of the ride **Snow White's Scary Adventures**, in which your wagon rolls through the dark forest as the Wicked Witch tries to waylay you in between attempts to catch Snow White. The addition of new scenes featuring the endearing Snow White has made this attraction less terrifying for youngsters.

➤ **The Many Adventures of Winnie the Pooh** is a popular addition to Fantasyland. Young children love to board the colorful honey-pot cars for a spin through the Hundred Acre Wood and familiar story scenes with A. A. Milne's characters as they encounter Heffalumps, Woozles, and a bit of blustery weather. Long lines are to be expected here.

A faster spin can be found on the giant, whirling tea-cups of the **Mad Tea Party**. You do get to help control the speed of the spin, but beware of dizzying effects of overzealous drivers in your cup. The idea originated from the 1951 Disney animated film of *Alice in Wonderland*.

Children won't want to miss meeting their favorite mermaid, Ariel, of Disney's film of Hans Christian Andersen's *The Little Mermaid*, at **Ariel's Grotto** across from Dumbo the Flying Elephant *(see page 31)*.

Mickey's Toontown Fair

When the ageless Mouse reached his 60th birthday in 1988, the first all-new land to be added to the Magic Kingdom was opened to commemorate the event. Then called Mickey's Birthdayland, its purpose was to offer everyone a chance to meet their favorite Disney stars – Donald Duck, Minnie, and, of course, the Big Cheese himself.

The land was later named Starland and, during the Walt Disney World Resort's 25th Anniversary in 1996, was renamed as **Mickey's Toontown Fair**. Dotted with whimsical circus tents, this colorful village offers youngsters a miniature roller coaster, a child-friendly play area, and plenty of character photo opportunities.

A fun way to arrive is via the Walt Disney World Railroad from Town Square or from the Frontierland Station.

Mickey's Country House gives an intimate glimpse into Mickey's private life. Through the back door, you'll find Mickey in the Judge's Tent signing autographs and posing for photos. **Minnie's Country House** gives a similar look at her home life and lets children listen to answering machine messages and peek into the refrigerator.

At the Toontown Fair in the **Toontown Hall of Fame**, visitors can admire the prize pumpkins and handsome lima beans.

The adventurous can explore **Goofy's Wiseacre Farms**, where **The Barnstormer** awaits. This small roller coaster modeled after biplanes wreaks havoc when it plows through Goofy's barn.

Tomorrowland

© DISNEY ENTERPRISES, INC.

Donald's Boat, the *Miss Daisy*, has enough leaks to cool everyone off. The Walt Disney World Railroad stops here on its way to Main Street and Frontierland.

Tomorrowland

This is the final stop on our clockwise journey through the lands of the Magic Kingdom, or a simple turn to the right if you've just arrived via Main Street. **Tomorrowland** is a glitzy, sci-fi-esque world, teeming with whirligigs, flying doo-dads, and whimsical architecture, lending the sector a Jules-Verne-crossed-with-Buzz-Lightyear look.

Children can have some fun driving the small cars of the **Tomorrowland Indy Speedway** around a twisting track. With an accelerator and brake, they have control of speed up to a modest maximum, but they don't have to look where they are going – the steering wheel is superfluous.

The Timekeeper promises a film experience allowing viewers to 'ride' along with Jules Verne on a time machine. The old Star Jets still whirl around a rocket-shaped tower, but the spiffed-up ride is now **Astro Orbiter**, featuring rotating planets installed on the top.

► Based on the 1995 Disney hit *Toy Story*, **Buzz Lightyear's Space Ranger Spin** can be enjoyed by children and adults. Cars are equipped with a joystick, a couple of laser cannons and electronic scoreboards. The idea is to help Buzz Lightyear save the universe from the evil Emperor Zurg by blasting as many of the bad guys as possible.

Walt Disney's **Carousel of Progress**, first shown at the 1964–65 New York World's Fair, has been refurbished with new figures and one reworked scene, and chronicles the way technology has changed the lives of an animatronic family. The open-air **Galaxy Palace Theater** stages regular musicals.

► **Space Mountain** is one of several rides that have remained virtually unchanged since it was installed. A perennial favorite, and deservedly so, this is the Magic Kingdom's most challenging coaster ride. Set on an indoor track, the ride is full of whiz bang visual effects and, weirdest of all, stretches of inky darkness. Check riding restrictions.

You can change your mind while you're waiting, and take a less harrowing ride on the **Tomorrowland Transit Authority**, a soothing, six-minute ride aboard trams, powered by non-polluting, electromagnetic linear induction motors, around the perimeter of Tomorrowland. Board near Astro Orbiter.

Epcot

Most people would guess that **Epcot** is an acronym, but few could say what it stands for. Walt Disney himself conceived the idea of an 'Experimental Prototype Community of Tomorrow' with one scheme comprising a huge transparent dome, sealing in a whole city of progress. Early in the planning, several international pavilions intended for a site next to the Magic Kingdom became the center of World Showcase in Epcot. Then Future World took off when large US corporations became excited by the concept and Exxon and AT&T (led by General Motors) signed on as sponsors.

Epcot has two entrances: the main one near Spaceship Earth – the great white 'golfball' visible for miles around – and International Gateway in World Showcase, intended mainly for those guests coming in from Epcot resorts. If you come by Disney bus, they'll drop you near the main

Monorail and Spaceship Earth, Epcot's distinctive landmark

entrance. The Disney monorail system links Epcot with the Magic Kingdom and its resorts by way of a change of train at the Ticket and Transportation Center (TTC).

From the Epcot resorts – Walt Disney World Swan, Walt Disney World Dolphin, BoardWalk, and Yacht and Beach Clubs – it's only a short walk or boat ride to International Gateway between the pavilions of France and the United Kingdom. If you come by car, you'll be directed to a place in the huge parking area. Rows are numbered and the zones are named, so write down your vehicle's location. Parking is free for guests who stay in Disney-owned accommodations. Others should keep their parking ticket, as it is valid for the whole day.

You'll need to buy a one-day ticket or a four- or five-day pass. Strollers and wheelchairs can be rented and, if in doubt, take into account the long distances you will have to walk to see this 260-acre (100-hectare) park; jokers say the Epcot acronym really stands for 'Every Person Comes Out Tired.'

The park is in the shape of a figure eight, aligned north to south. The main entrance is at the north end.

All the World's a Stage

All of the 50,000 people who work at Walt Disney World Resort are called 'cast members.' This is the entertainment business, the reasoning goes, and the rules that apply to the acting profession, apply here. Cast members wear 'costumes,' not uniforms. When they're in view of the visitors (the 'guests'), they're 'on stage.' There's no smoking or drinking. Actors would never wear 'out-of-context' jewelry or make-up, nor do members of the Disney cast. Make-up for women must suit the costume. Men sport no facial hair (with one or two exceptions – after all, Walt himself had a moustache).

A journey into space starts at Future World

Future World

This half of the figure eight illustrates the wonders of science and communications and the achievements of technology, with predictions for the future. Recent changes reflect greater awareness of environmental concerns. The human dimension is also more in evidence, with an increased emphasis on biology, medicine, health, and exercise.

Landmark of Future World, **Spaceship Earth** is a 180-ft (55-m) 'geosphere' made up of more than 14,000 aluminum and plastic triangles. The 'skin' is designed so that any rainwater falling on it is funneled inside and piped away to re-use for irrigation. During the busy season, this line can be long all day, as it is the first attraction most people see. You may want to wait until evening. The **Spaceship Earth** ride spirals upwards, tracking the history of human communication from cave drawings and Egyptian hieroglyphics to the invention of printing and beyond, before making a backward descent. The

Parades

Daily in the Magic Kingdom, the carnival-style 3pm parade, with five-story floats and countless Disney characters, makes its way from Frontierland down Main Street, U.S.A. Most evenings (at 8 or 9pm in summer with an extra show at 11pm on special nights) the Wishes parade travels along the same route. Replacing the long-running Main Street Electrical Parade, this event depicts Disney fantasy themes with a generous collection of lighting effects. The park hub in front of Cinderella Castle is one popular spot for watching. Another is Town Square – especially the Walt Disney World Railroad Station and station staircase – a better choice if you plan to leave the park right after the parade goes by.

The best viewing places are grabbed early, but the time it takes to secure them isn't worth giving up on a short visit. Fireworks set the sky ablaze above Cinderella Castle at 10pm when the Magic Kingdom is open late in summer.

twin curved buildings that used to house CommuniCore with its interactive exhibits have been refurbished and enlarged. Between the buildings is a computerized fountain that jets columns of water as high as 150ft (46m) into the air in time to music. This area, called **Innoventions**, features products at the cutting edge of technology. The two sections of Innoventions are:

Innoventions West, geared toward all ages with massive, state-of-the-art exhibits from Sega, IBM, and others.

Innoventions East, which has technological gizmos from GM and the popular Internet.Zone from Disney Online. Not to be missed are the toilet lids that automatically raise and lower.

The seven pavilions of Future World, including Spaceship Earth, form a circle, with gaps on the north side (the main entrance) and the south (where the two worlds of Universe of Energy join). To get to the first pavilion you should cut through Innoventions and keep going to the left.

Ellen's Energy Adventure: Ellen DeGeneres, star of the former prime-time television comedy *Ellen*, hosts this attraction with Bill Nye the Science Guy in an amusing take on the story of energy – from prehistoric days when oil was being formed to energy sources of the future.

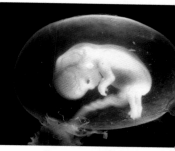

You can watch a fetus grow in The Making of Me

Wonders of Life: In the Met Life Corporation's gold-domed pavilion, Wonders of Life focuses on various aspects of biology and health. In **Body Wars**, you are 'miniaturized' to the size of a blood cell and propelled on a reckless motion-simulator ride through the human cardio-vascular system to fight a bacterial infection. Boarding restrictions apply.

Cranium Command is a humorous look at how a 12-year-old boy's mind and body learn to cooperate through a hyperactive day. Celebrities act the parts of the left and right sides of the boy's brain, and his heart, stomach, and adrenal gland.

The Making of Me sensitively explores all the wonders of pregnancy and birth by combining romance, cartoon spermatozoa competing to reach the egg, and remarkable live film of a developing fetus.

Interactive exhibits outside the theater offer a computer analysis of your golf stroke, a workout on video-enhanced exercise bicycles, and a review of the latest developments in medical technology. An improv group called AnaComical Players uses comedy to address health issues in another small theater.

But most people milling around this area are building the nerve to ride Epcot's newest attraction – **Mission: SPACE** – the only ride in all of Disney that offers you two chances to change your mind and provides a sick bag for those who should have taken the chance to get out when they had it. The interactive ride simulates a mission to Mars (each 'crew member' has a role to perform) and begins with a lift-off that gives you a g-force experience not dissimilar to what astronauts feel and ends with a seemingly weightless view of earth below you.

A Few Tips

- **Dress** is casual, but visitors must not go barefoot or bare-chested.
- You'll do quite a lot of walking and standing, so wear your most **comfortable clothing**, especially shoes, and watch out for sunburn.
- Do not bring your own **food and drink** into the theme parks. There are plenty of places to eat inside.
- Most indoor attractions forbid the use of **flash photography**.
- If you want to leave and return (even just to go to your car), be sure to have your **hand stamped** at the exit. You'll need your ticket as well.
- Carry **cash** for fast food and drinks, but most full- and counter-service places accept credit cards. Consider **sharing meals** with children to save money – portions often are very large.
- **Smoking** is allowed in designated areas only. Some non-Disney restaurants have smoking sections.
- If you rent a **stroller** (pushchair), tie a bright scarf or other piece of clothing to it so that no one takes it by mistake.

Test Track: General Motors has totally revamped the World of Motion pavilion, which used to take visitors on a placid chair ride through the history of transportation. The pavilion, which opened in 1999, featured the longest, fastest ride at Walt Disney World Resort – Test Track (with the cars approaching 65mph or 100km/h). The 1-mile (2-km) ride is based on a new car proving ground and travels both inside and outside the pavilion. Sitting six in a car, riders experience a five-minute race around a track of banked turns which takes them through cold, heat, sudden braking situations, and even a simulated crash.

A candidate for the Lost Children desk

Odyssey Center: Next to Test Track, the Odyssey Center houses the **First Aid and Baby Care Center** and a **Lost Children desk**. Here, you have reached the crossover of Epcot's figure-eight layout. You can make a detour into World Showcase, either on foot or in one of the boats that cross the lagoon, but in this guide we continue around the circle of Future World. If you want to do the same, either cut through Innoventions West, or take the walkway that runs along by the lagoon.

Journey into Imagination with Figment: This ride set in a blue-glass double pyramid, helps your imagination run wild as you take an eight-minute ride through a world of fanciful effects and illusions. Here, the 3-D movie *Honey, I Shrunk the Audience* is easily one of the most popular attractions at Epcot. Starring Rick Moranis of the 1989 hit film *Honey, I Shrunk the Kids*, this 3-D show with surprising special effects gives the audience that 'shrinking feeling' when things go awry for the famous inventor. Outside the theater, don't miss the fascinating 'jumping' fountains, where water springs from one pool to another.

The Land: This pavilion (by Nestlé) actually grows some of the food used in the park's own restaurants, such as the peppers used by Mexico's San Angel Inn and hydroponic salad greens used by The Land's own Garden Grill. **Living with The Land**, a boat trip, cruises through greenhouses set up to simulate a tropical rainforest, desert, the American plains, and a traditional farmstead.

Shark encounter

If you are especially interested in growing things, take the one-hour **Behind the Seeds** tour instead. You walk through the same areas and learn more detail. Numbers are limited, however, so make reservations early at the Green Thumb Emporium – through the gift shop near Farmer's Market food court. Starting every half-hour, the walk is guided by one of the agricultural staff members who explains some of the techniques.

Soarin' opened in 2005 to celebrate Disneyland's 50th anniversary. It simulates a majestic flight over California's stunning scenery including Yosemite and the redwood forests and ending where else, but at the birthday girl herself.

The **70mm Circle of Life** theater has a 20-minute motion picture based on characters from the hit 1994 movie *The Lion King*. Simba the lion, Timon the meerkat, and Pumbaa the warthog deliver a message on land use and the environment.

The Living Seas: United Technologies Corporation sponsors this experience, which claims to have the biggest saltwater aquarium in the world – 203ft (60m) in diameter, 27ft (8m) deep and holding more than 5 million gallons (18 million liters). Living among an imitation coral reef are more than 8,500 tropical fish, sharks, rays dolphins, and sea turtles from 65 species. You'll also get to see rescued Florida manatees.

You zigzag past a history of underwater exploration to board the **Caribbean Coral Reef Ride** through a submerged transparent tunnel. Then you can take as long as you like at the dual-level **Sea Base Alpha**, watching the fish and sea mammals, as well as divers working in the tank, close up. Research underway is explained by Living Seas scientists, and you can even try on a diving suit. At the Coral Reef Restaurant you can dine whilst enjoying a view of the colorful reef.

Disney's Town of Tomorrow

Epcot was originally conceived by Walt Disney as an experiment in urban planning – an Experimental Prototype Community of Tomorrow – but the plan was abandoned after his death in favor of a commercially viable theme park. The idea was revived in 1994 in the form of **Celebration**, a town designed from the ground up by Disney 'imagineers.' Numbering about 5,000 residents, it has a spotless downtown and houses designed by some of the most notable architects in the business. Celebration is 5 miles (8km) south of Disney World near the intersection of US 192 and I-4. For information, call (407) 566 2200.

World Showcase

The second 'circle' of Epcot, around the shores of World Showcase Lagoon, celebrates the culture and cuisine of 11 nations. Each 'country' is housed in a microcosm of its own striking architecture. In this guide we take a clockwise tour. Much of the fun of World Showcase (indeed all of Epcot) is in the entertainment sprinkled throughout. Check the daily schedule for showtimes.

Mexico: An ancient Maya pyramid looks as if it might suffer the fate of its original brethren in Yucatán and be overgrown by jungle greenery. All is cool, dark, and mysterious inside, with beautiful displays of pre-Columbian treasures.

At the rear of the pavilion, a boat trip on **El Rio del Tiempo** (the River of Time) meanders past an erupting 'volcano,' a film of an Aztec ceremony, an animated fiesta, an ingenious fiber-optic 'firework display,' and market-stall traders.

Norway: Oslo's 14th-century Akershus Castle, a turf-roofed cottage, a traditional wooden stave church, and 17th-century harborside houses from Bergen all inspired the pavilion's buildings.

Don't miss **Maelstrom**, the thrilling Viking longboat voyage which travels through Norway's myths and legends.

You disembark in a little port and see *The Spirit of Norway*, an inspirational short film that will make you want to visit the country.

China: Another fine collection of replica buildings centers on Beijing's circular Temple of Heaven, the perfect setting for showing a Circle-Vision 360° film travelogue, ***Reflections of China***.

Germany: The main attraction here is the **Biergarten**, with plenty of German food and loud, rousing music. Children love the model trains which run outside and beneath a charming bridge. For all the folksy image, the little toytown-like shops are engaged in real business: butter cookies at **Süssigkeiten**, wine tastings at **Weinkeller**, and crafts, beer steins, and cuckoo clocks at **Volkskunst**.

Italy: Beautifully detailed replicas of the Doge's Palace and the campanile re-create a miniature of the Piazza San

The Chinese pavilion centers on the Temple of Heaven

Eiffel Tower, Paris

Marco in Venice, complete with a gondola moored at the lakeside. Other buildings, statues, and gardens around the piazza are based on originals from various regions of Italy.

The American Adventure: You won't be surprised to find the host nation taking center spot at the head of World Showcase Lagoon. Presented by two of the most powerful US corporations, American Express and Coca Cola, two centuries of American history pass painlessly by in no more than half an hour in *The American Adventure Show*. It features several famous Audio-Animatronics figures, headed by Mark Twain and Benjamin Franklin.

Japan: The well-groomed gardens with their waterfalls, little bridges, and carved stone lanterns make a perfect retreat from the world around. The tall, stepped pagoda and 'flying roof' palace are based on the historic temples of Nara and Kyoto. The pavilion houses the **Bijutsu-kan Gallery** of traditional art, as well as the popular **Mitsukoshi Department Store** and several restaurants.

Morocco: As the only representative here of the Arab and Islamic worlds, Morocco takes its responsibility very seriously. Moroccan workers were hired to construct perhaps the most authentic of all the World Showcase buildings. Look out especially for the **Koutoubia Minaret**, a beautifully detailed prayer tower (the original is in Marrakech), and a reproduction of the Nejjarine fountain. The **Gallery of Arts and History** displays art treasures, intricate embroidery, and jewelry. In a re-creation of an ancient *kasbah*, artisans work with brass and silver.

France: Not surprisingly, gastronomy is the main theme here, and three superstar chefs (Bocuse, Lenôtre, and Vergé) are advisors to the restaurants. The big, five-screen, 18-minute travelogue ***Impressions de France*** will also whet your appetite for a trip. If you think you know the country already, think again. You'll hardly mistake the mini-**Eiffel Tower** for the real thing, but the rest of the architecture is a real *tour de force* in 19th-century Parisian style.

International Gateway: As Epcot began operations, it made sense to add quicker access to the park. Water launches run to and from Walt Disney World Swan and Walt Disney World Dolphin, BoardWalk, and Yacht and Beach Clubs, but the stroll along the waterfront path takes only a few minutes.

United Kingdom: Somehow designers have managed to compress a composite English village-town-city, with a dash of Scotland and Wales, into a living travel brochure. Architectural styles ranging from early Tudor to high Victorian are

---

Disney Cruises

Disney Wonder and Disney Magic are the two cruise ships operated by Disney. With 875 staterooms, they are modelled on luxury liners from the 1920s. They include seven-night land and sea vacations with three and four night stays at Walt Disney World Resort. They sail from Port Canaveral an hour east of Orlando, heading for the Caribbean and calling at Nassau, Freeport, and Castaway Cay in the Bahamas. A former rendezvous for drugs smugglers, the beautiful 100-acre (40-hectare) Castaway Cay was bought by Disney to turn into a vacation paradise for hiking, swimming, and snorkelling. Week-long cruises alternate between the eastern and western Caribbean, with a stop at Castaway Cay.

included in convincing detail. **The Rose & Crown** pub feels like home to British visitors – and the beers are as authentic as they can be, after being pasteurized and served cold to suit American laws and tastes. A live band, British Invasion, plays Beatles hits in the garden courtyard.

Canada: Inspired by the Château Laurier in Ottawa, **Hôtel du Canada** is the landmark. Massive though it looks, even close up, it's really not much bigger than a good-sized house. *O Canada!* is a Circle-Vision 360° film that takes you from coast to coast through the great outdoors. You'll wish you had 360° eyes, too.

Disney-MGM Studios

Celebrating the American love affair with movies, this combination theme park and film and tape production set opened in 1989. Emulating Hollywood in the 1930s, its Art-Deco streets lead you to real and replica sets. Animated films are produced here, as well as live-action film and television programs, and often you can watch the action through windows into the studio areas.

If you come by car, signs are easy to follow from the I-4 or US 192 highways. Parking is free for guests of Disney accommodations. Others should keep their parking ticket – it's valid all day. If you are staying at one of the Epcot resorts, you can come by water launch. Check the park's closing time, which varies from 7pm onwards.

Touring the Studios

Once through the gates, you may feel as if you're in a California dream. Some real fun can be had as soon as you hit **Hollywood Boulevard**, where a troupe of costumed actors draw guests into the act. Where Hollywood Boulevard intersects with **Sunset Boulevard**, you'll see a huge 'tip' board on the right chalked with news about show times, ride waits, and special events. Frequently, film or television celebrities make appearances in a motorcade and in an on-stage 'conversation' with their audience. Details are printed in the daily *Entertainment Schedule*.

Check the schedule of the **Theater of the Stars** along Sunset Boulevard for the times of the live stage musical based on Walt Disney Pictures' 1991 animated hit, *Beauty and the Beast*.

Just behind this venue is the seating for **Fantasmic**, Disney-MGM's big finale that is loaded with special effects and pits Mickey Mouse against Disney's most unsavory characters. Another show based on a Disney animated feature, *Voyage of The Little Mermaid*, runs continuously at Animation Courtyard.

Not for the faint-hearted – The Twilight Zone™ Tower of Terror

© DISNEY ENTERPRISES, INC.

Rides and Attractions

At the end of Sunset Boulevard, the newest sector of Disney-MGM Studios, created in the mid-1990s, stands one of the tallest structures in Walt Disney World Resort. Resembling a decaying Hollywood hotel, the structure houses **The Twilight Zone Tower of Terror**. Guests begin their ride through the eerie Fifth Dimension based on the famous TV show **The Twilight Zone**. They then ride to the top of the building, where the elevator breaks loose and plunges 13 stories. It's a sudden and – for a few seconds – terrifying fall before the elevator shoots skyward and tumbles again.

Just around the corner, the high-speed **Rock 'n' Roller Coaster** starring Aerosmith also has a high scream factor. Travel from 0–60mph (0–97km/h) in 2.8 seconds while Aerosmith tunes blast away.

The **Chinese Theater**, which stands behind Mickey's Sorcerer's Hat – the park's icon – is a full-size replica of the historic **Mann's Chinese Theatre**, where movie stars' footprints and handprints are set in cement – here they've done the same.

Inside the theater, the 20-minute **Great Movie Ride** sends you on a slower-paced twisting track through vivid scenes from *Casablanca*, *The Wizard of Oz*, *Raiders of the Lost Ark*, and several more classics. Life-like Audio-Animatronics figures of stars and some realistic special effects supplement the footage.

Also at Disney-MGM Studios is **Sounds Dangerous**, which gives visitors a chance to create the sound effects that add realism to a show or film.

Creating the Magic

'Don't they mind being watched?' Everyone on **The Magic of Disney Animation** tour wants to know how the artists feel, working under the gaze of thousands of visitors each day. The answer is 'yes and no.' Loss of privacy is balanced by the fact that these animators are being acknowledged instead of hidden in a back room. There's no doubt the balance has succeeded: the many artists here have created millions of drawings for Disney films that include *Beauty and the Beast*, *Aladdin*, and *Mulan*.

Act out a role

Check your schedule and plan the best time to head to the vast open-air theater where the **Indiana Jones Epic Stunt Spectacular** is performed several times a day. You should plan to get here and choose a seat before showtime – the closer you are to the stage, the more you will feel the special effects. The show is

Harrison Ford in *Indiana Jones*

live, on three movable sets, and you may have a chance to join in. 'Extras' are chosen from the audience before the show starts.

At **Star Tours**, a battered *Starspeeder* space-craft with *Star Wars* characters C-3P0 and R2D2, as well as robots with questionable skills, suggests that all might not be as smooth as the space travel agency claims. As you board for a trip to the Moon of Endor, you're welcomed by a loony captain; then the thrills begin as you experience the 'virtual reality' of a runaway ride, in which film and simulator movements are perfectly synchronized. Check boarding restrictions before riding.

Jim Henson's Muppet Vision 3-D is a clever film and special-effects experience for adults and children. Objects appear to fly straight toward you. Sensory effects, fiber optics and Audio-Animatronics figures of Muppet characters, as well as 'live' ones that enter the audience, keep the action coming throughout the 25-minute show.

Honey, I Shrunk the Kids Movie Set Adventure is a great place to let the children burn up some energy. Based on the film of the same name in which a scientist accidentally minia-

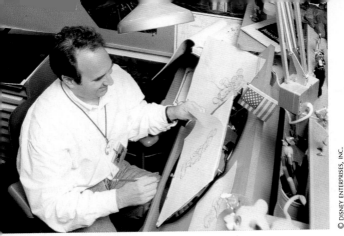

In the animation studio

turizes his and the neighbors' children to the size of ants, the attraction mimics what it might be like to roam through a forest of 25ft (7.5m) blades of grass and meet insects big as houses. Small children can climb 'spiders' webs' and slide down tubes of foliage or an outsize roll of discarded 'film.'

Behind-the-Scenes Tours

➤ Avoid lunchtime or evening when you visit **The Magic of Disney Animation**. You are more likely to see artists at work during normal working hours. The starting point is in the Animation Courtyard behind the Hollywood Brown Derby restaurant. Much of the tour is a self-guided walk, beginning with a short and hilarious film, *Back to Never Land*, a lesson in the basics of animation featuring Walter Cronkite and Robin Williams.

Next comes a real animation studio where you can take your time to move along, looking through the windows and over the shoulders of artists. You'll see what goes on in each department. As a finale, you'll watch sequences from famous films including *Bambi* (Walt Disney once admitted that this film was his particular favorite), *101 Dalmatians*, and *Cinderella*.

The best examples of the animator's art have come to be recognized as modern classics, and connoisseurs pay high prices for them. Original 'cels' once sold for a few dollars each, but they now can fetch several thousand dollars. In the **Animation Gallery**, you'll see examples for sale.

The afternoon is probably a good time to go on the excellent **Disney-MGM Studios Backlot Tour**, beginning across from the Studio Catering Co. near the *Honey, I Shrunk the Kids* play area. The 20-minute shuttle ride takes you first through costuming and scene building, then past stored props and old cars, and even old aircraft. **Residential Street** is an outdoor set with some backless 'houses' that may look familiar from films and TV.

Then, watch out! In **Catastrophe Canyon** you get a memorable look at the artificial floods, fires, and explosions that gave disaster movies their name. If you're sitting on the right side, you may get splashed, and on the left you definitely will, so cover your camera. Incidentally, it takes only 3½ minutes to recycle the 70,000 gallons (318,000 liters) of water and to have the catastrophic chain of events ready for a replay.

You can break off the tour at this stage, or follow Roger Rabbit's pink, painted footsteps to **Inside the Magic: Special Effects and Production Tour**, a walking

Traveling with young kids? Then go to <www.disneyworld.com> and order a free preschooler vacation planning video and guide. Tips include the best child-friendly rides. Older children can practice their cartoon skills on <www.disney.go.com/activities>

tour that takes 45–60 minutes to complete. You'll see how hurricanes and sea battles are simulated in a tank, and you can look down into three real working sets: Soundstages I–III. Check the Entertainment Schedule to see what may be going on, and which stars might be around.

Two more showbiz attractions are on Mickey Avenue. **Who Wants to be a Millionaire – Play It!** is a faithful recreation of the television game show, though contestants win Disney swag instead of cash. **Walt Disney: One Man's Dream** is a movie on the life and career of the man who started it all.

Eat with the Stars

The restaurants in the Studios are also part of the show. **The Hollywood Brown Derby**, Hollywood Boulevard, has a Wall of Fame of caricatures. Talk-a-likes of the famous gossip-column queens, Louella Parsons and Hedda Hopper, might well be at one of the tables. At **The 50's Prime Time Café** you can eat while vintage sitcoms play on television. **The Sci-Fi Dine-In Theater** serves up sandwiches and 'monstrous' salads while you sit in booths that look like 1950s convertibles and watch science-fiction B-movies from the same period.

DISNEY'S ANIMAL KINGDOM

Opened in April 1998, this extraordinary theme park is the most expansive of the Disney domain: Five times larger in area than the Magic Kingdom and almost twice the size of Epcot, Disney's Animal Kingdom encompasses the African savannah, an Asian rainforest, a mountain retreat, and the age of the dinosaurs.

Disney's Animal Kingdom Lodge has its own 35-acre (14-hectare) wildlife reserve, so you can watch the animals from your room. Otherwise, early in the morning is the best time to arrive at the park to see the animals.

The Oasis

As your point of entry into this botanical wonderland, the Oasis offers a tranquil spot to prepare for wild safari adventures and miraculous time travel. Admire the exotic flora and fauna of this lush tropical garden, with cool mists enshrouding idyllic waterfalls and pristine glades. Attentive visitors will find within the miniature landscape unusual animal life and startling, fragrant flowers.

Discovery Island

Encircled by the **Discovery River**, this central station serves as an island gateway to the rest of Disney's Animal Kingdom. The village is dominated by the 145ft (44m) **Tree of Life**, the symbolic heart of the park. With a canopy wider than the tree is tall and a trunk stretching more than 50ft (15m) wide at its base, the Tree of Life is a striking icon,

A close encounter with some gorillas

Tigers on the prowl

lavishly decorated with 325 hand carvings of animals. Within the tree is a digitally enhanced theater showing a 3-D animated film, *It's Tough to Be a Bug*, based on the Disney/Pixar hit *A Bug's Life*.

DinoLand U.S.A.

Devoted to everyone's favorite extinct creatures, this area of the park is the location of **DINOSAUR**, where you'll travel back 65 million years, just in time to rescue a dinosaur from doom as a meteor crashes into the Earth. More than two dozen state-of-the-art, Audio-Animatronics creatures simulate the dinosaur realm, while computer-controlled motion effects and moving motion-simulator vehicles pitch you to and fro. It's an intense, thrilling ride that visitors often want to repeat.

Children run the show at **The Boneyard**, Disney's best interactive playground featuring an open-air archeological dig. The young ones can dig for dinosaur bones and other fossils, climb on T-rex and various other remains, swoop down twisting slides, and give parents a chance to rest their own bones.

Before exiting beneath the 50-ft (15-m) Brachiosaurus, you'll enjoy wandering through **Chester & Hester's Dino-Rama**, a motley assortment of carnival-style games implementing every dino-trick in the book. If you are looking to pick up gifts for the kids, **Chester & Hester's Dinosaur Treasures** store is overflowing with dino-related toys.

Just behind The Boneyard lies **Theater in the Wild**, a 1,500-seat amphitheater featuring one of the park's 'don't miss' live shows, complete with high-flying acrobatics, **Tarzan Rocks!**, based on the 1999 Disney movie, *Tarzan*.

Africa and Rafiki's Planet Watch

Here, a real adventure begins. First, stroll the streets of Harambe, meet cast members from Africa, and soak up the authentic sights and sounds of an East Kenyan coastal village.

Stop in at Conservation Station via the **Wildlife Express**, a replica 1890s train, for more information about Disney's efforts to care for its prized collection, and meet the park's excellent veterinary staff.

Next, set off on the **Kilimanjaro Safaris**, where you'll prowl over 100 acres (40 hectares) of open land in search of adventure. The wildlife preserve is filled with varying terrain, from thick, densely wooded forests to picturesque rivers and rolling hills. Don't forget to bring along the camera, as you'll encounter some breathtaking animal life. Riding in open-sided cars, you will pass within a jaw's snap of Nile crocodiles, and your vehicle may have to wait for rhinos or giraffes crossing the path.

Other attractions in Africa include the **Pangani Forest Exploration Trail**, where you can stroll to the lush grounds of lowland gorillas, see hippos from an underwater portal, and explore an aviary with many rare birds.

Asia

This land in Disney's Animal Kingdom was added to the park in early 1999 and rounds out the attractions with another big ride – **Kali River Rapids**. You are sure to get wet on this thrilling whitewater raft adventure with an eco-logical message. Wear a swimsuit with T-shirt, then change afterward for comfort.

The bats and tigers are a big draw on the **Maharajah Jungle Trek**. At **Flights of Wonder** on the Caravan Stage, birds of prey and other species amaze the 700-member audience with close-up demonstrations of their natural behaviors.

WATER PARKS

Note that during bad weather water parks such as Typhoon Lagoon and Blizzard Beach may close.

▶ Typhoon Lagoon

Faced with the competition of other water parks round

The Circus Comes to Downtown

One of the latest Disney attractions is the first permanent home for the Canadian performance spectacular, **Cirque du Soleil**. The purpose-built $27 million 'tent' in Downtown Disney, next to Typhoon Lagoon, has a resident troupe of around 70 performers. With trapeze artists, acrobats, and clowns, fabulous sets and flamboyant costumes, this is no traditional big-top act. (The Montreal-based company has six troupes altogether – two others are based in Los Angeles, the other three are on permanent tour.) Though it might seem a long way from Main Street, U.S.A., the show's high entertainment value caught the Disney imagination. Some of the acts are avant garde, with male trapeze artists in tutus and outbreaks of opera singing, but children are often more ready to appreciate new experiences than their parents, and it makes a great family show. There are two 90-minute performances a day, five days a week. At around $60 an adult, tickets are more expensive than the entrance fees to any of Disney's four theme parks, but satisfied customers claim it's worth it.

Typhoon Lagoon's biggest draw is its giant Surf Pool

Orlando, Disney responded with this heavily themed park. Here, you can rent towels and take in your own food and drink (no alcohol or glass allowed), though food is available at two restaurants. The park is imaginatively landscaped: In a 56-acre (22-hectare) South Sea island setting you can forget you're miles inland: There's even a white-sand beach for basking, and plenty of shade trees. The main attraction is the giant **Surf Pool**, a lagoon with a wave generator that sends out perfect, 6ft (1.8m) bodysurfing rollers across the 2½-acre (1-hectare) pool.

Mount Mayday, rising 90ft (27m) above the lagoon, has the wreck of a shrimp boat, the *Miss Tilly*, perched convincingly on its peak as if cast there by a passing tidal wave. From over 50ft (15m) up the slope, a couple of giant water slides – **Humunga Kowabunga** – send you screaming at 30mph (50km/h) through a tunnel to plummet into the lagoon. It's not for very small children, and there are restric-

Be prepared for a cooling-off period

tions. For a gentler but still exciting ride, you can hop on the rubber inner tubes through the white water cascades of **May-day Falls** and **Keelhaul Falls**, or go four at a time down Gangplank Falls.

For a Zen-like ride, grab an inner tube and let **Castaway Creek** float you gently along, circling the park and meandering through woods and grottoes. You can snorkel over **Shark Reef**, an artificial coral reef with shoals of real fish and even some small (and harmless) sharks as companions. For the very young, **Ketchakiddie Creek** has paddling pools, small slides, and fountains. If you forgot to bring swimwear, **Singapore Sal's** has a good selection, as well as sun protection cream and other beach essentials.

Blizzard Beach

Disney's newest water world takes a different approach to the water park theme – one that is decidedly chillier. This

66-acre (26-hectare) 'ski resort' surrounds **Mount Gushmore**, which swimmers may ascend via chair lift. 'Liquid ice' slopes and water-filled toboggan runs are the main attractions here.

Inner-tubers can idle along **Cross Country Creek**, a 2,900-ft (800-m) trough encircling the entire park. **Snow Stormers** pitches its victims down three flumes that switch back through slalom-style gates. The main attraction on Mt Gushmore, **Summit Plummet**, simulates a ski-jump tower, from which the adventurous face a nearly vertical drop to the base of the mountain. Approaching speeds of 55mph (86km/h), swimmers let loose screams of terror and pleasure.

OTHER DISNEY ATTRACTIONS

Not to be missed by sports fans is **Disney's Wide World of Sports** complex, which hosts the Atlanta Braves baseball team for spring training, the Harlem Globetrotters basketball team's winter training sessions, and Orlando Rays minor league baseball. The 7,500-seat baseball stadium is part of a busy athletic complex featuring six basketball courts, training rooms, softball fields, 12 tennis courts, a golf driving range, and facilities for about 30 other sports. It is also the venue for numerous amateur and professional competitions. This 200-acre (80-hectare) site gives Disney a huge realm devoted to sports-related attractions.

The NFL Experience, a football program designed mostly for kids, is offered daily. The complex is just west of I-4 on Victoria Way, near Disney-MGM Studios. Call (407) 939 1500 for a list of upcoming events.

Shopping opportunities

Downtown Disney sprawls along the shore of Lake Buena Vista about a mile east of Epcot. It provides a wide variety of dining, entertainment, and shopping and is covered in more detail on pages 92–3.

Pleasure Island, nearby, is another night-time entertainment complex. There is an admission fee after 7pm, which covers all eight clubs (guests under 18 must be accompanied by a parent or legal guardian; Mannequins and BET Sound-Stage™ do not admit persons under 21 years old). Smaller in scope and more sedate is **Disney's BoardWalk**, with buskers, ice-cream stands and gingerbread architecture.

UNIVERSAL ORLANDO RESORT

Disney's main competitor in Orlando is more hi-tech and brasher than the original, but it also has accommodations so visitors can spend several days here without stepping outside. Once known only as **Universal Studios Florida**, Universal expanded dramatically in 1999 into two theme parks and a sprawling dining and entertainment complex with three hotels: the original Universal Studios Florida, the thrill mecca Islands of Adventure, and, between the

---

Universal vs Disney-MGM Studios

Which movie attraction should you choose: Universal Studios Florida or Disney-MGM Studios? Universal Studios is a lot bigger (which doesn't just mean more of the same). It doesn't have the cozy, Hollywood-in-its-heyday feeling of Disney-MGM Studios. More Universal attractions are based on contemporary films, though Hitchcock is represented. Several of Disney's movie attractions are based on classics or cater to the younger crowd. The streets and sets of Universal Studios are on a grander scale, so there's more walking, but it does have some of the most thrilling rides you'll experience anywhere, though they might scare small children. True film fanatics will want to head for both Disney-MGM Studios and Universal.

two, serving as a gateway for visitors arriving by car, Universal CityWalk.

The original Universal Studios park bills itself as the 'biggest film and TV production facility east of Hollywood.' Your feet will believe it after a full day here, which you'll need to experience some thrilling rides and shows. North of International Drive and signposted off the I-4 highway, it's easy to find by car. As with all parks, make a note of where you leave your car.

Arrive before the 9am opening hour, collect a guide leaflet and map at the gate, determine your priorities, and beat the rush to one of the popular attractions. Near the end of each day, visitors take up positions for the fireworks display, an explosive show on the lagoon with plenty of firepower.

The Incredible Hulk Coaster travels 150ft in under 3 seconds

This guide takes you through the park in a roughly clockwise order, but the route you choose may be different as you head for your objectives. Near the main entrance you'll find production information about what's happening in the studios or on the sets.

Cartoon characters
At **Production Central** – straight ahead down **Plaza**

of the Stars and right where it starts at the crossroads – you'll find the Neutron Adventure featuring Nickolodeon's Jimmy Neutron, Boy Genius. Guests file into a move theater equipped with several rows of motion simulators. What follows is a mad cap tour of Nickolodeon's cartoon universe in a spaceship piloted by Jimmy, who has to save the world from wicked egg-shaped aliens known as Yokians.

In **Nickelodeon Studios** you can tour the working television studio where such favorites as *Double Dare* are produced. The itinerary varies, but you are likely to get a glimpse of the wardrobe and makeup departments, see stage sets and watch actors in rehearsal. Whether you will be able to watch the actual taping of a broadcast depends on what's in production when you visit. Tickets are available on a first-come, first-served basis. Call (407) 224 6355 for scheduling information.

Shrek 4-D is a multisensory experience that picks up the story of the softhearted ogre where the 2001 animated film left off. The images are enhanced by special effects built into the theatre itself.

The rolling attraction **Twister …Ride it Out** features a monster tornado based on the 1996 feature film. At five stories high, the cyclone whips up immense volumes of air,

---

Universal Information

Universal Orlando Resort, 1,000 Universal Studios Plaza, Orlando, FL 32819-7610.

Information: (407) 363 8000, <www.universalstudios.com>

Reservations: 888-U-ESCAPE (837 2273).

Opening times: 9am to 6–10pm, depending on the season.

Entrance fees to the two attractions are around $50, with dscounts for 3–10-year-olds.

Laurel and Hardy are among the street stars

while beating rains and a deafening roar complete the terrifying experience.

Revenge of the Mummy is Universal's newest ride, which spent over 10 years in development. It is set indoors and billed as a psychological thrill ride, taking full advantage of set design, high-speed coaster tricks and optical illusions to scare you again and again.

Clustered around one end of The Lagoon, **San Francisco/ Amity** features sets of Fisherman's Wharf and Amity (*Jaws*) Harbor, snacks and seafood, and two outstanding attractions.

Earthquake – The Big One puts you in a San Francisco subway train sitting quietly at a station when the quake begins. The thrill measures 8.3 on the Richter scale.

The other big event is **Jaws**. Yes, he's back – and he's out to get you. Take the boat ride that almost ends in disaster as the 32-ft (10-m) great white shark attacks relentlessly (with a bit of help from special effects and advanced technology).

Men in Black Alien Attack

World Expo has the last word in rides, however. The dynamic, time-traveling **Back to the Future ...The Ride** takes flight-simulator technology to great heights of realism and scale. While you are thrown about in eight-person DeLorean-shaped vehicles, the special effects and pictures are wrapped around you on monster hemispherical screens. Your manic journey through time sends you careering over Ice Age glaciers, blasting through a volcano, and disappearing down a dinosaur's throat.

Men in Black: Alien Attack is a ride 'n' shoot-the-aliens attraction with laser guns for every guest. The more aliens you zap, the higher your score. The only hitch is that the aliens shoot back, sending your vehicle into a wild tailspin with every hit.

Children's attractions

Woody Woodpecker's Kidzone is a well-designed space devoted to younger children, with attractions that include the kiddy-sized thrill ride **Woody Woodpecker's Nuthouse Coaster** and **Curious George Goes to Town**, a large and busy wet and dry play area based on the prankish monkey in H.A. and Margaret Rey's popular kids' books.

Kiddy fun includes **Fievel's Playland**, an interactive

adventure based on the 'American Tail' films, and a sing-along musical show, **A Day in the Park with Barney**, that ubiquitous purple dinosaur popular with the toddler set, and a host of other friends. At **Animal Planet Live**, secrets of training dogs, cats, and birds to 'act' are revealed. **ET Adventure** is a gentle journey on a star-bike to help ET's home planet, with nice special effects.

Woody Woodpecker

Hollywood is a 1950s street set in chrome and pastels. Among the shops and cafés is the **Gory, Gruesome and Grotesque Horror Make-Up Show**, the funniest attraction at the park. The show features a wisecracking special-effects expert and a straightman, who offer a short course on the finer points of stage blood, rubber knives, explosive squibs and other staples of the horror genre. After the show, you can stop for a burger across the street at **Mel's Drive-In** (from George Lucas's 1973 *American Graffiti*).

Terminator 2: 3-D Battle Across Time is a virtual adventure, a film and special-effects showcase in which 3-D images are projected onto 180° of 70mm action. The 12-minute film is based on the 1991 blockbuster starring Arnold Schwarzenegger, Linda Hamilton, and Edward Furlong, and includes footage shot especially for this attraction.

Islands of Adventure

Ride and attraction technology pushes the virtual envelope at this second Universal Studios Escape theme park, opened in 1999. Islands of Adventure, which has Steven Spielberg as creative consultant, wraps its thrills in clever theming that runs the gamut from *The Cat in the Hat* to *Jurassic Park*.

From the moment you collect your park brochure, strollers, and whatever else you need at **Port of Entry**, your escape into exotic adventure begins. Taking the clockwise tour around the park, you'll begin where super heroes and villains do battle.

On **Marvel Super Hero Island**, don't miss one of the park's most thrilling rides, **The Amazing Adventures of Spider-Man**, which pits Spiderman and park guests against sinister foes in a high-tech, action-packed comic-book battle. Skip lunch or wait at least an hour after eating to board the stomach-churning **Doctor Doom's Fearfall** and **The Incredible Hulk Coaster**.

Cartoon craziness prevails in the comic-strip world of **Toon Lagoon**. Take the plunge on **Dudley Do-right's Rip-**

The Incredible Hulk Coaster

saw Falls flume ride, based on episodes of *Rocky and Bullwinkle*. A whitewater raft adventure, **Popeye & Bluto's Bilge-Rat Barges**, promises a wild ride and a soaking, too.

'Dinomania' reaches new dimensions in **Jurassic Park**, the prehistoric island based on Spielberg's popular film. Thrills begin with the interactive **Jurassic**

The Cat in the Hat

Park River Adventure, where state-of-the-art creatures roam and a T-Rex gives riders a scare. An 85-ft (26-m) flume plunge sets a new theme-park record as the longest, fastest, steepest. There's a great climbing spot for children at **Camp Jurassic**. **Jurassic Park Discovery Center** and the calmer **Pteranodon Flyers** round out this area.

The Lost Continent is a wonderful, watery world. Embark on a voyage beneath the sea and get caught in a battle between Poseidon and Zeus in **Poseidon's Fury**. Their weapons: more than 350,000 gallons (1,597,400 liters) of water and exploding balls of fire. **Dueling Dragons** is not for the faint of heart. The inverted roller coaster includes near-misses with riders on the opposite track. Restrictions apply. Stationary thrills can be found at **The Eighth Voyage of Sinbad** stunt show.

Would you ride it with a cat? Would you ride it with a hat? You will soon be creating your own Seuss-like rhymes after making a trip to **Seuss Landing**, including **The Cat In The Hat** ride based on Dr Seuss's many children's books and characters. Don't miss this spot if you have young children in tow. The **Caro-Seuss-l** is an elaborate twist on the popular

Bob Marley – Tribute to Freedom

carrousel, and **One Fish, Two Fish, Red Fish, Blue Fish** offers a whimsical interactive ride. The **If I Ran the Zoo** playland is a child's interactive paradise with an animal theme.

Universal CityWalk

This 12-acre (4.5-hectare) entertainment complex brings a great deal of excitement to Universal's bursting-at-the-seams attractions. **CityWalk** introduces a wealth of state-of-the-art spaces designed for live music, dancing, and gourmet celebrity restaurants, all of which are based on the CityWalk complex at the Universal Studios Hollywood theme park in California.

Among the attractions at CityWalk's vibrant promenade is **Bob Marley – A Tribute to Freedom**, devoted to the Jamaican musician and cultural icon.

The first **Hard Rock Live Orlando** with the world's largest Hard Rock Café replaces the original Hard Rock Café at Universal Studios Escape. The dining area is based on the architecture of the Forum in Rome, and includes Hard Rock's first live-music venue, a 2,200-seat club. Dine and see the show under one roof.

Also at CityWalk, among the numerous nightclubs, specialty shops, and a wide variety of eateries, are the **Universal Cineplex**, a 20-screen, 5,000-seat theater complex, **Jimmy Buffett's Margaritaville**, with Buffett's own brand of island music-and-cheeseburgers-in-paradise setting, and **Emeril's Restaurant Orlando** by the renowned chef from New Orleans.

SEAWORLD ORLANDO

Marine parks are a Florida tradition, and SeaWorld Orlando is the biggest and best (7007 SeaWorld Drive; open 9am to 6–10pm; entrance fee). **Shamu**, the friendly killer whale featured on the park's logo, is the star, but the many other attractions here could easily entertain and painlessly educate you all day. If you have only two or three hours, it's still worth the trip.

Near the south end of International Drive, look for Sea-World exit signs from the I-4 highway. Plan your visit with the map and schedule you get at the gate. Near the entrance, you can change money, rent lockers, wheelchairs, or strollers in the shape of dolphins, and ask about special tours.

Throughout the park you can feed many of the sea animals in their habitats.

A killer whale at SeaWorld

The Shows

At **Shamu Stadium**, on the far side of the park's big lake, the star's extended family of killer whales entertains visitors several times a day in cleverly choreographed shows, **The Shamu Adventure** and, at night, **Shamu Rocks America**. These are must-see events, and the large seating area fills up well before showtime. Spectators sitting in the front 10 or 12 rows can expect to get splashed – if not completely soaked – by some of the almost 6 million gallons (20 million liters) of salt water in the tank. As much as you'll admire the agility and gentleness of the whales, you'll also marvel at the skill and balance displayed by their trainers.

Other amazing animal behaviors are displayed at **Key West Dolphin Fest**, where Atlantic bottlenose dolphins entertain guests in a beach-themed area.

Aware of public concern about the ethics of keeping and training captive animals, SeaWorld Orlando emphasizes its role in conservation and research, and supports several 'green' causes. In the shows, the trainers go out of their way to stress the care that is taken of the cast.

Clyde and Seamore Take Pirate Island at the Sea Lion and Otter Stadium is a swashbuckling misadventure with clever performances by a comical cast of sea lions, otters, and a huge, hairy walrus.

Other shows at SeaWorld: **Blue Horizons** is set on the lagoon; **Odyssea** is an underwater fantasy world full of acrobats, mimes, and dancers at the Nautilus Theater; and **Pets Ahoy**, with a crew of pets rescued from animal shelters and trained to do silly skits.

Ride Attractions

To up the thrill factor and stay competitive with Disney and Universal, SeaWorld Orlando has added several 'white-knuckle' rides. The latest, **Journey to Atlantis**, is a water-coaster thrill ride through the lost city of Atlantis. Boats plunge a staggering 60ft (18m) on a nearly vertical drop into the ocean, only to surface after enduring hair-raising twists and turns through tidal waves. Along the way, holograms and LCD images bring the whole drama of the fabled lost city to life.

Wild Arctic has been a favorite attraction for several years. Riders in a virtual helicopter are tossed around in a simulator while viewing an exhilarating film featuring crashing glaciers and an avalanche. Afterward, you stroll through the icy realm of an Arctic 'base station,' **Pacific Point Preserve**, to view live polar bears, 3,000-lb (1,360-kg) beluga whales, and other animals of the region.

Kraken is billed as the fastest, tallest, and longest roller coaster in Orlando.

Polar bears in the Arctic 'base station'

Other SeaWorld Attractions

Some of the best things can be seen at practically any time of the day, mostly without a wait. In **Tropical Reef**, you stand in the cool darkness facing thousands of colorful fish in a huge, brilliantly lit aquarium. Outside once again, you can feed the harbor seals in one pool, and touch the stingrays in another.

On a hot and sticky Florida day you will envy the residents of **Penguin Encounter**, a large tank refrigerated to the Antarctic chill that penguins prefer. Almost five tons (more than 4,000kg) of snow falls here every day. As you drift by on a moving walkway, the glass walls let you see the residents hilariously marching and slipping on the rocks and ice, then zooming away underwater.

Shark Encounter is a children's favorite, showcasing a monstrous collection of various species of vicious-looking sharks and venomous fish. The winged moray eels are fascinating as they glide through the tank. Viewers are safely housed in a long, transparent underwater tunnel, with 6-in (15-cm) thick walls.

From underwater to high up in the sky, you can ride to the top of the needle-like 400-ft (122-m) **Sky Tower**, well worth the small charge if only for the marvelous view.

> **Backstage tours and other special programs cost up to $400. Small groups can find out how to care for polar bears, seals, whales, and dolphins. The Trainer for a Day program pairs visitors and trainers for a full day with killer whales and dolphins.**

Several backstage tours, including the **Trainer for a Day Program** and the **False Killer Whale Interaction Program**, cost extra.

Discovery Cove

SeaWorld Orlando broke ground in 2000 with a new theme park, **Discovery Cove**, touting an intimate, reservations-only experience of water activity among a variety of fish and mammals. The price is substantial for a day at this park, which includes swimming and playing with dolphins, snorkeling among tropical fish, and feeding and holding tropical birds. Visitors check in at a concierge desk and are promised no waiting in lines.

Wet 'n' Wild

You may have thought there are only a certain number of ways you can climb steps, board a slide, and splash into a shallow pool. Here they have thought of all those, and then some – there are now at least 14 different slides and rides.

At 6200 International Drive (at Republic Drive, exit 30A south of the I-4 highway), **Wet 'n' Wild** is convenient to reach (open daily 9 or 10am to 5–11pm depending on the season; entrance fee).

Going down a treat

Again, keeping up with the obligatory thrill factor, the park has a line-up of nerve-tingling slides and rides: **The Black Hole**, where you cork-screw down in total darkness, carried by a flow that's fed by almost 5 tons (4,000kg) of water a minute; **Bomb Bay** where riders climb up to a compartment shaped like a large bomb and are then maneuvered over a six-story waterslide; and the **Hydra Fighter**, an interactive water thrill where riders aim water pump guns at each other. Young children get to have their fun, too, at the **Kids' Park**.

Stomach churner

The six-story **Flyer** sends its four-passenger toboggan careening through steep, banked curves. Equally thrilling is a stomach churning tube ride known as **The Surge**, while **The Storm** has you dropping from an elevated chute into a giant open bowl where you spin in circles to a splash landing. The latest attraction is **Disco H$_2$0**, where you swirl round an aquatic nightclub to the sounds of the '70s. Life-guards are always nearby. Wave machines generate regular 4-ft (1.2-m) rollers for body-surfing in a big pool. For a more tranquil ride, you can meander along **Lazy River** on a rubber tube.

Hotshots on the Hydra Fighter

It's all a great way to cool off and take a break from the 'dry' theme parks. The obvious question is: How does Wet 'n' Wild compare with Disney's Typhoon Lagoon *(see page 58)*? The answer is, Wet 'n' Wild offers more, and wilder, slides, so if you're looking for pure thrills, this is the place to be.

Typhoon Lagoon, on the other hand, has more beach, more shade, and a bigger wave pool.

DOWNTOWN ORLANDO

Downtown Orlando, so often overlooked by tourists, offers some first-class art, museums, and a welcome respite from the crowds and prices of the resorts.

The **Orlando Centroplex** is the name given to a group of Orlando's biggest venues: Tinker Field and the Florida Citrus Bowl located near Lorna Doone Park and the TD Waterhouse Center, Bob Carr Performing Arts Center and the Expo Center all located near Lake Dot.

The **TD Waterhouse Centre** is home to the Orlando Magic – the city's professional basketball team – and other sporting events. The **Bob Carr Performing Arts Center** puts on concerts, touring ballet, Broadway productions, and opera, and the **Citrus Bowl** is a football stadium seating 70,000. Built in 1936, this is one of the oldest stadiums in the US and has the lion's share of college football history to tell, as it often hosts the national Championship match. **Tinker Field** is a small baseball stadium used for spring training and minor league games. **The Expo Center** caters for Orlando's booming conference trade.

Some of the area's affluent suburbs sit just north of here. At **Loch Haven Park**

Orlando skyline with Lake Eola

Tales of the unexpected at Gatorland

(take exit 43 off the I-4 for Princeton Street and go east for 1.6km/1 mile) stands the **Orlando Museum of Art** (2416 North Mills Avenue, open Tue–Fri 10am–4pm, Sat–Sun noon–4pm; entrance fee). It hosts the temporary blockbusters that tour nationally, and loan exhibitions alternate American and African art. But its greatest strength is its Art of the Ancient Americas Collection, with pre-Columbian pieces dating from 2000 BC to AD 1500.

Another time frame, BD (before Disney), persists in **Winter Park**, a posh district where wealthy northerners came to spend the winter as long ago as 1890. Now the millionaires' mansions are joined by chic restaurants, stylish hotels, and fashionable shops. **The Morse Museum of American Art** (445 North Park Avenue; open Tue–Sat 9.30am–4pm, Sun 1–4pm; entrance fee) is a magnet for lovers of Art-Nouveau glass, and home to an unrivaled collection of Tiffany lamps, vases, and beautiful windows rescued from the fire which destroyed the home of Louis Tiffany (1848–1933, son of the jewelry maker, Charles) on Long Island in 1957.

Inhabiting a stylish modern building, the **Orlando Science Center** (777 E. Princeton Street; open Mon–Thur 9am–5pm, Fri–Sat 9am–9pm, Sun noon–5pm; entrance fee) offers 11 exhibit halls of the latest in technological wonders, plus planetarium shows in its large-format movie theater, the **Cine Dome**. The **Crosby Observatory** is open on Friday and Saturday evenings for star-gazing. Intriguing exhibits take you through the human body, Florida's eco-system and a tour of the solar system. The **DinoDigs** exhibit features dinosaur fossils and allows visitors to join an excavation site. A great place to take your children on a rainy afternoon.

Kissimmee

An endless ribbon of highway lined on either side by billboards, motels, gas (petrol) stations, T-shirt outlets, and other tacky tourist traps doesn't hold out much hope on the way to Kissimmee. Is there a real Kissimmee? Where's the little cattle town founded in 1880? Not at **Old Town**, a modern pastiche with food outlets, amusement rides, and specialty shops, on route US 192 at No. 5770, near I-4.

You'll find traces of original Kissimmee along Broadway and Main Street. There's still a livestock auction each Wednesday morning (at 805 East Donegan Avenue), and a great rodeo takes place here each February and October.

Giant alligator jaws herald the entrance to **Gatorland** on route 441 near Kissimmee (14501 South Orange Blossom Trail; open daily 9am–dusk; entrance fee). The serious purpose of this place is farming the 5,000 alligators and crocodiles that reside here. The fun is in watching a man wrestle with a gator, or the beasts leaping for raw chickens in the **Gator Jumparoo**. Precious little of the alligators is wasted; you can taste deep-fried gator snacks ('you've seen the show, now eat the cast'), and buy various accessories made from their skins.

On the gentler side, a terrific attraction for families with young children is **Green Meadows Petting Farm**, (1368 Poinciana Boulevard; daily 9.30am–4pm; entrance fee) where kids get to milk a cow, mix with the pigs, chickens, and goats, and take a hayride.

EXCURSIONS FROM ORLANDO

Cypress Gardens

Go west on the I-4 highway toward Tampa, then take the US 27 exit south and follow signs to Winter Haven, then head right at Waverly and go along route 540 for about 5 miles/ 8km. (2641 South Lake Summit Drive, Winter Haven; open daily 9.30am–5pm; entrance fee).

An easy 40-mile (65-km) drive southwest from Orlando, near the old-established resort of Winter Haven, this 223-acre (90-hectare) lakeside park began as a botanical garden in the 1930s, making it central Florida's oldest theme park. Now it's more famous for its spectacular **water-ski shows**. World champion performers do balletic lifts, acrobatic stunts, human pyramids, and circus clown routines.

The noisy water-ski show contrasts with the usual calm of the gorgeously manicured gardens and the **southern belles** in crinoline dresses and hooped petticoats who stroll among the flowers and sit twirling their parasols.

The **Sunshine Sky Adventure** is a circular platform on a mechanical arm, which raises a new load of passengers 153ft (46m) every few minutes. It's worth being up here during one of the water-ski shows.

Back on the ground, **Southern Crossroads** is a replica of an old Florida country town from around the year 1900. A

Cypress Gardens aquatic stars

dazzling array of butterflies awaits you in the **Wings of Wonder Butterfly Conservatory**, where more than 1,000 of the dazzling creatures from 50 different species flit about this lovely enclosed greenhouse.

Electric boats take you on waterways that wind through the gardens' different environments, while guides tell you about the 8,000 species of plants as well as the wildlife. There's probably not enough to keep you here for a whole day, but it's a lovely diversion that might be combined with a visit to Bok Tower Gardens.

Bok Tower Gardens

Continue past the Cypress Gardens exit on US 27 for 5 miles (8km), exit on route 17A to Alt. US 27, then turn left on Burns Avenue for about 1½ miles (2.5km).

Florida's highest hill may be only 324ft (99m) above sea level, but it does stand out from the flat landscape near Lake

Wales, southwest of Orlando. It became even more of a landmark when Edward Bok, a Dutch-born New York writer and publisher founded a 128-acre (52-hectare) nature reserve and garden here and topped it with an elegant 205-ft (62-m) belfry. Built of pink-and-gray marble carved into a blend of Gothic and Art Nouveau, the octagonal **Bok Singing Tower** houses a 57-bell carillon which rings a variety of gentle tunes every half-hour. At 3pm on most days a live carillonist plays a 45-minute recital of hymns, folk tunes, and classics.

The tranquil gardens and pleasant, shaded forest walks make an idyllic contrast to the nearby theme park world.

Space Coast

From Orlando take the Beeline Expressway–Route 528 – east directly to Cape Canaveral. (Open daily 9am–dusk except certain launch days; entrance fee. Groups of 10 or more children can arrange an overnight adventure at the Kennedy Space Center, when they will meet an astranaut, see IMAX films and have guided tours. For information, call (321) 449 4444. To find out when the next launch is scheduled, check the newspaper, call (800) 572 4636, or check the website <www.KennedySpaceCenter.com>).

It's an easy 50-mile (80-km) drive due east to Titusville from Orlando (via a small toll) to the coast, where America's astronauts are launched into space. **The Kennedy Space Center** sent the first mission to land a man on the moon in 1969. Once home of the early NASA launches, today it is the home of the space shuttles. Since the tragic loss of Space Shuttle Columbia in February 2003, there has been only one space shuttle launch, but it's still well worth visiting the **Kennedy Space Center Visitor Complex** since other space craft such as rockets and explorers are still launched here. The Rocket Garden includes several of the earliest research vehicles and also the kind of rockets that put the first Ameri-

The Space Shuttle Columbia

cans into orbit. In a significant blend of technology and sculpture, the Astronauts' Memorial honors those who have died in space program accidents. Multi-media exhibits and shows explain the technology of space travel, and a chunk of real moon rock is on display.

A favorite for children is the **Astronaut Encounter** program where they are able to meet a genuine astronaut who can tell them what it's like taking a journey into space.

There are several ticket packages to choose from. The basic visit includes the bus tours and IMAX films. Join the line for tickets early, planning what you want to do before you reach the ticket window. **The Kennedy Space Center Tour** includes highlights of the moon landing program, stops at an observation tower with a bird's-eye view of the shuttle launch pads, and gives a peek into the International Space Station center, where modules are being completed for future launches.

Busch Gardens birds

Astronauts used to relax, swim, and surf at **Cocoa Beach**, the strip of island to the south of the Kennedy Space Center. You can do the same, though the resort is bigger now; the dunes also make an excellent viewpoint for watching launches.

Busch Gardens

Take the I-4 highway west to Tampa and exit at I-75. From the I-75 take exit 54 and follow the signs.

A 70-minute drive from Walt Disney World Resort, in a huge 300-acre (120-hectare) park northeast of Tampa, beer giant Anheuser-Busch has built a theme park with a mix of lush landscaping, quaint rides and shows, heavily themed play areas, and monster thrill coasters. Much of the theme is early 20th-century Africa, with more than 3,400 animals to view, as well as authentic Moroccan-style architecture.

Park sections include (clockwise from entrance) **Morocco**, **Bird Gardens**, **Land of the Dragons**, **Stanleyville**, **Congo**, **Timbuktu**, **Nairobi**, and **Myombe Reserve**. To the right of Myombe are **Edge of Africa**, **Serengeti Plain** and **Egypt**. Grab a map at the entrance, as the layout can be confusing.

Serengeti Plain is a main attraction. This 80-acre (32-hectare) open site, with big-game animals and herds of grazing zebras and antelopes, is viewed from cable-cars or an old-fashioned train.

At the **Great Ape Domain** on the Myombe Reserve, you can hear the call of the wild. Lowland gorillas and chimpanzees reside in a recreation of their natural environment – take the self-guided tour.

Beyond the animals, you can get a drenching on the **Congo River Rapids** whitewater raft adventure or go screaming down the **Tanganyika Tidal Wave**, with a 55-ft (17-m) drop. At **Stanley Falls**, a log flume ride remains popular. Then you can turn your world upside down on the **Kumba**, **Montu**, **Python** or **Scorpion** (the tamest) – four death-defying roller coasters. **Gwazi** is Florida's largest and fastest twin dueling roller coaster on an old-fashioned wooden track, while **Land of the Dragons** is filled with gentle water-play attractions and kiddy rides.

Busch Gardens' state-of-the-art white-knuckle ride is **SheiKra**, where riders drop straight down at 70mph (112 km/h) before hurtling along an underground tunnel.

Entrance to Gwazi Coaster at Busch Gardens

There are several musical shows, a Rhino Ralley and a birds of prey display. After all the excitement, you can visit the on-site brewery and sample the beers at **Hospitality House**.

Adventure Island

About 1 mile (1.5km) from Busch Gardens, **Adventure Island** is a water park that offers waterfalls, waterslides, waves, and the **Aruba Tuba**, a 420-ft (128-m) tunnels slide.

The park closes in winter and in the fall is open weekends only.

WHAT TO DO

You may think there's quite enough to occupy you in Orlando's theme parks. But there are activities both inside and outside the parks that you may easily overlook.

SPORTS

Watersports are a year-round pleasure in Florida's delightful climate. Even in winter, the sun will tempt you out on most days, and the swimming pools will always be warm. Add plenty of golf courses, tennis courts, fishing spots, and a host of other sporting facilities and you have a recreation retreat.

Boating, Canoeing, and Water-skiing

The Walt Disney World Resort has a web of waterways connecting lakes large and small, and almost all of its resorts are on a lake or canal, with their own landing places or marinas. Dozens of different types of pleasure craft can be rented.

For **sailing**, conditions are best at two big lakes (Seven Seas Lagoon and Bay Lake at the Magic Kingdom resorts). Single hulls and catamarans are available at several Disney resort hotels. The same locations also have speedboats, drivers, and all the equipment necessary for **water-skiing**.

The canals around Fort Wilderness are good for **canoeing**, and you can take **pedal boats** on the lakes. If you prefer a motor to do the work, take a mini-speedboat, a gentler motorized raft, or rubber boat.

Outside the Walt Disney World Resort, several resort hotels have lakes and watersports opportunities, or check with your hotel guest services desk for local boating information. One of the loveliest passive cruising experiences is

Water-skiing at Walt Disney World Resort

the **Scenic Winter Park Boat Tour**. Or, rent a canoe in beautiful Wekiwa Springs State Park east of Orlando off I-4.

Fishing

Fish flourish in Florida's many lakes and canals thanks to careful stocking and strict environmental policies. Guests at the Walt Disney World Resort are usually surprised to find that fishing is allowed from the shores at **Fort Wilderness** and in the canals by **The Villas** at the Disney Institute (but it is, of course, carefully controlled).

In addition, organized fishing expeditions leave daily from **Bay Lake**, starting off at 8am and in late morning and mid-afternoon. Reservations are required and the cost is quite high, but chances are good that you'll catch sizeable bass. Tackle, bait, and refreshments are provided.

Outside the Walt Disney World Resort, Florida freshwater lakes and rivers are abundant: try **Lake Tohopekaliga** (or Toho) in Kissimmee. Or drive east on I-4 to Wekiwa Springs State Park for a delightful canoeing experience or a swim in the cool spring.

Golf

Walt Disney World Resort's five 18-hole championship courses enjoy a great reputation with professionals and amateurs. A 9-hole walking course is intended for families and novices, but it is also used by more experienced golfers.

> **When Walt Disney World Resort opened two new courses in 1992, it became the biggest golf resort in Florida, earning it the nickname 'Magic Linkdom.'**

Fees are relatively high for Florida (reduced if you can start after 3pm, March through September, or 2pm October through February), but facilities are generally excellent. The **Magnolia** and **Palm** courses sit just across from the Polynesian Resort near the Magic Kingdom, with the 9-hole Oak Trail course adjoining the Magnolia. The **Lake Buena Vista** course, a little narrower and shorter, is near the Disney Institute.

The newer **Bonnet Creek Golf Club**, in wooded country just north of Port Orleans-Riverside Resort, has the **Eagle Pines** and **Osprey Ridge** courses. Although each course has its own character, they're all par-72 and play about 7,000yd (6,400m) from the championship tees. Just because some bunkers are shaped like Mickey's ears doesn't make them any easi-

Golf courses abound in the Orlando area

er to escape – Disney courses have long been used on the US pro tour. You can rent or buy anything you need for a game of golf at each club's pro shop. Lessons with resident professionals also can be arranged. For those who take their golf a little less seriously, there are two miniature courses, **Fantasia Gardens** and **Winter Summerland**.

Outside the Walt Disney World Resort, Orlando has plenty of other golf courses. Try the **Hyatt Regency Grand Cypress** or the **Marriott World Center** resort hotels as well as several country clubs, such as the **Orange Lake Country Club** in Kissimmee, and **Timacuan Golf and Country Club**, Lake Mary.

Swimming

Apart from the **water parks** (Typhoon Lagoon, *see page 58*, and Blizzard Beach, *see page 60*), every resort and hotel in the Walt Disney World Resort has at least one pool. Many are imaginatively themed around ruined pirate forts, beached ships, grottoes and mountains, and have fun slides for the children.

Ballooning over the lakes

Then there are the **beaches**. The Walt Disney World Resort may be an hour's drive from the sea, but the lakeside resorts have fine, white sandy shores, shady trees, lounge chairs and cabanas – and the lake water is pure and clean. Lifeguards are on duty (if not, there will be a sign notifying you of their absence). Disney hotels' pools or beaches are open only to guests staying at Disney-owned accommodations, but many other resort hotels have excellent facilities and most budget hotels or motels will have some sort of pool.

Outside the Walt Disney World Resort, the water park **Wet 'n' Wild** *(see page 75)* makes for an excellent day out; **Cocoa Beach**, south of Cape Canaveral, has a fine beach with yearly surfing championships; and further south, making up just one segment of the 160km (100 miles) of beaches, you'll find **Satellite Beach** and **Indialantic Beach**, which will be less crowded.

Tennis

More than two dozen tennis courts are scattered around the Walt Disney World Resort – at the **Grand Floridian**, **Contemporary**, and **Fort Wilderness** resorts; between the **Walt Disney World Swan** and **Walt Disney World Dolphin**, at the **Yacht** and **Beach** clubs; and at the Disney Institute **Villas**. You can make a court reservation anytime from 7am to 7pm. If you want to improve your strokes, sign up for lessons with the pros at one of several Disney resorts. Outside the Walt Disney World Resort, the big hotels and country clubs all have courts. Try the **Orange Lake Country Club** in Kissimmee, or the **Magic Athletic Club** in the RDV Sportsplex.

Other Activities

Jogging and Cycling The most scenic routes at Walt Disney World Resort are around the lake at Caribbean Beach, the Crescent Lake promenade at the Yacht and Beach clubs, and at Fort Wilderness. You can rent bicycles at Caribbean Beach, Dixie Landings, Port Orleans, BoardWalk, Coronado Springs, and at the Disney Institute. Bicycles are only to be used in the area where they are rented. Be aware that bicycling on Orlando sidewalks is prohibited.

Health clubs and spas complete with state-of-the-art exercise machines and pampering treatments are provided at many resorts in and around Orlando. Disney's two first-rate spa and fitness centers are the Spa at the Disney Institute and the Grand Floridian Spa. The Winter Park area offers Euro Day Spa & Salon, with mud packs, massage, and even a 'spa du jour.' Most of the finer resorts offer fitness centers.

Trail riding on placid horses is offered at Fort Wilderness and Poinciana Riding Stables at Kissimmee. You can go walking and bird-watching along Fort Wilderness's nature trails, or ice-skating at Orlando Ice Skating Palace or the RDV Sportsplex.

SHOPPING

Many shops are inside the theme parks, side-by-side with the attractions; in fact, sometimes they are attractions themselves. The shopping opportunities don't end there:

At **Downtown Disney** in Lake Buena Vista, acres of shops are arranged along the waterfront and are open daily.

Most of the shops within Walt Disney World Resort are designed to sell gifts and souvenirs or more expensive collectibles. Close to Walt Disney World Resort are several shopping centers including Crossroads of Lake Buena Vista, situated at the end of Disney's Hotel Plaza Boulevard. Here, you'll find an excellent supermarket with a delicatessen counter, a café and pharmacy, bookstore, bank, shoe, and clothing shops, and several restaurants in the moderate price range.

Shopping is no problem in any of the Orlando parks and resorts

For serious clothing shopping, you'll need to take a trip outside of the Walt Disney World Resort to one of the monster **Orlando shopping malls** featuring many of the famous-name stores.

> **Once Upon A Toy in Downtown Disney is a 16,000 sq ft toy store, which is teamed up with the Hasbro toy company. Buy a Mr. Potatohead and mix and match the cartoon characters' features.**

The closest of these is Florida Mall on Sand Lake Road, east of International Drive. Fashion Square Mall is close to downtown Orlando on East Colonial Drive. Old Town in Kissimmee has many shops in among the restaurants and entertainment facilities. Park Avenue in Winter Park, north of Orlando, has fashionable shopping.

Discount and 'factory outlet' malls are worth a visit, if you have the time to rummage through 'pile-'em-high-sell-'em-cheap' stocks to find what you want. Try Belz Factory Outlet Mall and Quality Outlet Center, both off International Drive. A crop of well-run discount shops has taken root a few miles south of the Crossroads shopping area on SR 535.

ENTERTAINMENT

Entertainment oozes from every corner of the Orlando-Kissimmee area. Check the tabloid *The Weekly* or *The Orlando Sentinel*, especially on weekends, for full listings of concerts (rock, pop, or symphony), ballet, opera, and theater by local or touring groups.

If you have the energy to **dance** after a long day at the theme parks, several clubs and discos operate until around 2am. **8 seconds** (Livingston Street) is a rodeo bar with a mechanical bull and country dance lessons. The Social (Orange Avenue) has an historic ambience but is often filled with corporate events.

Dinner Shows

Food and entertainment packages at an inclusive price are all the rage in the Orlando vacation belt, and some of Disney's resorts offer their own versions. You don't have to stay there to go — you simply need a reservation. That may not be easy for the popular **Hoop-Dee-Doo Musical Revue** at Fort Wilderness Campground, which offers family-style 'country cookin' and three nightly shows of energetic song, dance, and comedy in Wild West style.

The **Polynesian Luau** at the Polynesian Resort is the kind of show you might expect to see in Hawaii, with South Seas cuisine adapted to American palates.

Outside the Walt Disney World Resort, dinner shows are more raucous, fueled by unlimited beer or wine. Prices are competitive, there's plenty to eat, and service is efficient.

Options include: **Medieval Times** (Highway 192, Kissim-

Boogie woogie piano at Pat O'Brien's in Orlando CityWalks

mee), a jousting tournament with expert horsemanship; **Sleuths Mystery Dinner Shows** (8267 International Drive, Orlando), where the murder plot is even thicker than the stew; and **Arabian Nights** (Kissimmee, W. Irlo Bronson Memorial Highway), starring horses, acrobatic riders, and chariot races.

> **You must be 18 or older to get into nightclubs and 21 or over to be served alcohol. Carry your passport (or US driver's license) as proof.**

Downtown Disney/Pleasure Island

When Disney does night-time entertainment, it's with the same panache and attention to detail as you'll find in the theme parks. **Downtown Disney and Pleasure Island** are the great night-time escapes, with a first-rate mix of theater, dining, shopping, and live music. Cirque du Soleil, the critically acclaimed theatrical circus, performs an original show twice a day, Wednesday to Sunday. **House of Blues**, **Wolfgang Puck Café**, **DisneyQuest** indoor virtual reality complex, plus eclectic shops add grit to the mix. At Pleasure Island bars, discos, comedy acts, and live bands rev up nightly through 2am. During the day you can visit the area free of charge; after 7pm a Pleasure Island ticket covers entry to all nightclubs.

Disney's BoardWalk

In an effort to keep up with its visitors' craving for nightlife, Disney has created a number of entertainment complexes, sporting clubs, restaurants, bars, and shops. At BoardWalk, across Crescent Lake from the Yacht and Beach Club Resorts, the dance scene continues at **Atlantic Dance**, where swing dancing has caught on fire. Those who cannot bear to miss the big game will find comfort at **ESPN Club**, where more than 70 monitors broadcast up-to-date scores, post-game commentary, and instant replays (even in the rest rooms). Eating in front of the TV is mandatory. **Jellyrolls** features dueling grand pianos, and **Big River Grille & Brewing Works** was Disney's first brew pub.

Universal Studios CityWalk

A great collection of restaurants, clubs, and theater can be found at CityWalk. **Hard Rock Live Orlando, Jimmy Buffett's Margaritaville**, and the **Latin Quarter** are just some of the spots to check out. **CityJazz** features live performances and the famous New Orleans watering hole, **Pat O'Brien's**, brings its equally famous 'Hurricane' drink to Orlando. **B.B. King's Blues Club** on the second level of CityWalk offers food and live music every night.

The world's largest Hard Rock Cafe, CityWalk, Orlando

Films

If you're looking for some more relaxing entertainment, all the latest movie releases (not only Disney's) are at the 24-screen AMC complex at Downtown Disney West Side. Other state-of-the-art complexes are located at Universal Studios CityWalk, Pointe Orlando on International Drive, and in the Disney city of Celebration. Ticket prices are generally lower for early evening shows.

Orlando Area Calendar of Events

Depending on the time of year you visit, you may wish to take in one of central Florida's many annual special events.

January Cypress Gardens' Poinsettia Festival & Garden of Lights (through January 10); The Walt Disney World Marathon (with 5km course for childen); Indy 200 auto race.

February Black History Month Festivals at Disney and throughout the area; Mt Dora Arts Festival (one of the first weekends in February); Mardi Gras at Downtown Disney and Universal Studios Florida; Silver Spurs Rodeo in Kissimmee.

March Bay Hill Invitational Golf Tournament; Winter Park Sidewalk Art Festival.

April Orlando-UCF Shakespeare Festival downtown; Orlando International Fringe Festival downtown (check listings in *The Orlando Sentinel*).

May Epcot International Flower & Garden Festival; Zellwood Sweet Corn Festival. Star Wars weekends at Disney-MGM Studios.

June Florida Film Festival at the Enzian Theater in Maitland and other theaters (check listings in *The Orlando Sentinel*). Unofficial Gay Disney weekend.

July Lake Eola Picnic in the Park July 4; Fourth of July celebrations throughout Walt Disney World Resort; Wet 'N' Wild Summer Nights.

August Cypress Gardens' World Precision Hang Gliding Tournament.

September ABC Super Soap Weekend at Disney-MGM Studios with day-time drama celebrities. Official Disneyana Convention, Epcot.

October Food and Wine Festivals at Church Street Station and Epcot; Silver Spurs Rodeo in Kissimmee; Walt Disney World Golf Classic; Pleasure Island Jazz Fest; Halloween Horror Nights at Universal Studios Florida or other theme-park Halloween events.

November Festival of the Masters art show at Downtown Disney; Holiday events at all theme parks.

December Rockin' holiday events at all theme parks; Maceys parade at Universal Studios; Christmas in the Park in downtown Winter Park; New Year's Eve extravaganzas downtown and at all theme parks.

EATING OUT

Florida is a major producer of beef, fish, shellfish, and vegetables and is a world leader in growing citrus fruit. Fierce competition means you'll usually get good value for your money, especially in the type of food America does well: steaks, barbecues, broiled fish, and fried chicken, combined with a buffet or salad bar. See the list of recommended restaurants on pages 135–142.

In the past, theme parks were accused of dishing up only fast food laced with fat and sugar. Now, in response to the adverse publicity, the choice is more varied. The old faithfuls are still available, but the overall style is more healthy, with plenty of salads, fresh fruit, and frozen yogurt as well as ice-cream. Buffets and full-service restaurants in the theme parks and hotels cater to mainstream tastes but have become more adventurous, and, especially in Disney territory, the décor and theming are half the fun.

The Magic Kingdom
A few restaurants in the Magic Kingdom offer priority seating arrangements (tel: 407-WDW-DINE or through Disney Guest Services): Cinderella's Royal Table in Cinderella Castle, Tony's Town Square, and Liberty Tree Tavern. If you're in a hurry, the Crystal Palace is a convenient cafeteria near Main Street, and Cosmic Ray's Starlight Café is one prominent quick-service operation. You'll find fast-food dining all over the park.

Epcot
You wouldn't go to the Magic Kingdom just to eat, but you might do so at Epcot. Future World has the usual counter-service locations as well as two full-service restaurants, but the

difference at Epcot is that each of the 11 countries serving national dishes in World Showcase runs at least one restaurant.

Future World

The two full-service restaurants here are The Land pavilion's Garden Grille and the Coral Reef Restaurant in The Living Seas pavilion.

World Showcase

In **Mexico** the San Angel Inn, overlooking the River of Time boat ride, is an offshoot of a famous Mexico City restaurant, though the spices are mild compared to the original cuisine. The informal Cantina de San Angel by the lagoon has quick-service tacos, tortillas, and beans.

In the **Norway** pavilion the Restaurant Akershus puts on a magnificent buffet, including salted and spiced herring, hot

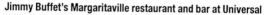

Jimmy Buffet's Margaritaville restaurant and bar at Universal

Chef Emeril Lagasse at Emeril's Restaurant Orlando

and cold entrées, Norwegian cheeses, and delicious desserts.

Nine Dragons restaurant in the **China** pavilion offers various regional styles which range from spicy Szechuan to the more familiar Cantonese cuisine.

In the **Germany** pavilion the Biergarten has *wursts*, dumplings, sauerkraut, roast meats and big steins of beer, as well as yodelers, musicians, and dancers.

L'Originale Alfredo di Roma Ristorante in **Italy** runs the mouthwatering gamut from pastas to *gelati*.

Liberty Inn flies the flag for basic, quick-service **American** burgers, french fries, and old-fashioned apple pie. Plans are currently in the works for a finer dining experience in the American Adventure, too.

In the **Japan** Teppanyaki Dining Rooms, you sit around a flat grill where a chef stir-fries the food of your choice. In the eateries here, you'll find light, deep-fried seafood and vegetables, grills, and sushi.

Morocco's Marrakesh restaurant features couscous and kebabs, roast lamb, and sweet honeyed desserts accompanied by musicians and a belly dancer.

In **France**, the Chefs de France is an airy room with a fantastic view of the World Showcase promenade. The fare is among the best at Epcot, with menus created by famed French chefs Paul Bocuse, Roger Vergé, and Gaston Lenôtre.

The **United Kingdom** is represented by the traditional-style Rose & Crown Pub where you can fill up with fish and chips, steak and kidney pie, and trifle.

Le Cellier in the **Canada** pavilion is a popular stop with its maple-glazed salmon, roasts, and Canadian specialties.

Disney-MGM Studios

Here, the food is all-American – even the Italian and the chili – served up amid entertainment themes. You can schedule priority seating for the four full-service restaurants *(see pages 135–39)* at their doors.

Elsewhere in Walt Disney World Resort

Although the clubs at **Downtown Disney Pleasure Island** don't open until 7pm, restaurants throughout the three Downtown Disney areas – West Side, Pleasure Island, and Marketplace – operate from 11am.

At the **Marketplace**, Cap'n Jack's Oyster Bar is a fine place to watch the sunset. The menu offers excellent crab cakes, garlic oysters, and other sea specialties. Rainforest Café is one of the best family dining experiences, heavily themed with Animatronics animals and special effects. The food is great, too. Fulton's Crab House is a fine seafood restaurant, with fresh fish flown in daily, on board the anchored riverboat *Empress Lilly* (named in honor of Walt Disney's wife, Lillian). At the **West Side**, choices include the House of Blues restaurant and music hall and Wolfgang Puck Café, by the world-famous chef. The **Crossroads at Lake Buena Vista** has a good selection of non-Disney food outlets. A line-up of excellent restaurants on International Drive, at Universal Studios Escape, and in and beyond downtown Orlando will tempt vacationers, as well.

HANDY TRAVEL TIPS

An A–Z Summary of Practical Information

A

ACCOMMODATIONS (See also YOUTH HOSTELS and the selection of RECOMMENDED HOTELS starting on page 127)

In high season reservations may be hard to come by, especially at Walt Disney World Resort. Book far in advance. State taxes are extra *(see page 118)*.

American hotels/motels usually charge by room rather than number of occupants. Most rooms have two double beds, a private bathroom, and color television. 'Efficiencies' are rooms with kitchenette or separate kitchen and dining area, with dishes, pans, and cutlery.

Peak periods in Orlando are: mid-December to early January; February to April (including Easter); and early June to mid-August. At other times, prices are slightly lower at some Disney accommodations and may be much lower at non-Disney properties.

Some resort hotels offer special rates to guests who dine on the premises. Inquire about package deals, often including breakfast and dinner, when making reservations.

Larger and deluxe hotels employ a concierge who can arrange tours, call a taxi, or rent a car for you. Visitors on a budget can economize by making their own arrangements.

AIRPORTS

Orlando (McCoy) International Airport (code MCO) is 9 miles (15km) south of downtown Orlando and about 25 miles (40km) from Walt Disney World Resort. Spacious, glittering, and constantly expanding, it has three terminals, with satellite gates reached by 'peoplemover' shuttle trains. Disney characters often make appearances during the day.

Ground transport *(see also page 125)*. Taxis and less expensive shuttle minibuses ply between the airport and Walt Disney World Resort locations, International Drive, downtown Orlando, Kissimmee, and Cocoa Beach. Some hotels operate free shuttle services to and from the airport; if you are on a package tour, airport transfers may be included. There's a public bus to downtown Orlando.

Check-in time. Arrive at least two hours before domestic and three hours before international flights. For flight information, telephone your airline.

Other Florida airports. Miami, Tampa, Fort Lauderdale, West Palm Beach, and Key West also have international airports.

Domestic flights. Air travel is by far the quickest and most convenient way of getting around the US. Travelers from abroad can buy a Visit USA ticket, which gives substantial discounts and sets no fixed program. To benefit, you must buy these before you enter the country or within 15 days of arrival.

Fares change constantly, so it's wise to consult travel agents for the latest on special deals.

B

BICYCLE RENTAL

Bicycles are available for hire at several Disney accommodations including Fort Wilderness, Caribbean Beach, Dixie Landings, and Port Orleans Resorts. Locks are included.

C

CAMPING

Camping American-style often involves recreational vehicles (RVs) such as campers, motor homes, or caravans (trailers). If you are camping this way, Woodalls publishes the most comprehensive guide, which lists and grades campgrounds and their facilities. ('Campsite' in the US means the specific spot where you put your RV or tent.) Camping by the road or on private land without permission is both illegal and unsafe.

Disney's Fort Wilderness Resort has sites where you can put up a tent or park your trailer or RV. Reservations required.

CAR RENTAL/HIRE

Competition keeps rates relatively low. Reserving a car before you arrive is often cheaper. Rental companies operate at all of Florida's bigger airports.

You are advised to ensure you have CDW (collision damage waiver), or you will be charged for repairs, regardless of whose fault the collision is. Many holiday packages promise a free car, but you usually have to pay Florida taxes and CDW when you collect it.

To rent a car you must be over 21 (sometimes 25) with a valid driver's license. Some agencies make exceptions for 18-year-old drivers paying by credit card. For tourists from non-English-speaking countries, a translation of the driving license is recommended, together with the national license or an International Driving Permit.

It is generally more convenient to pay with a credit card than with cash. Sometimes cash is refused at night and weekends.

CHILDREN

Orlando's theme parks and Florida in general offer enough to make the area a child's paradise. The rides themselves are appealing, but so are the hotel pools, game rooms, organized youth activities, and crowds of their peers.

In the parks, walking distances are quite long, but strollers are available for rent. The sun, heat, and humidity can take their toll, especially during long waits for popular attractions. Always apply sunscreen to children. Small and nervous children could be disturbed by some rides; take advice from the staff. Even the famous Disney characters can seem frightening to the very young. It might be worth warning children that the characters don't speak! Younger children may find stressful the following rides in the theme parks: the Magic Kingdom's Space Mountain, Big Thunder Mountain Railroad, and Splash Mountain; Epcot's Mission: Space; Disney-MGM Studios' Star Tours and The Twilight Zone Tower of Terror; Universal Studios' Back to The Future, Jaws, and Twister; and SeaWorld's Journey to Atlantis.

Restaurants cater to guests of all ages, and many of the larger hotels provide services specifically for children, for example babysitting, play groups, and special entertainment.

CLIMATE

Winter is usually delightful in central Florida, but there are rainy and cold spells – temperatures can dip to freezing. On the other hand, winter temperatures can reach 80°F (30°C). It's best to pack clothing for layering if temperatures drop.

Summer ranges from hot to very hot, with high humidity. From June to October, it rains briefly most days. Despite the number of recent hurricanes, on average, Florida is hit hard by a hurricane or tropical storm one year in seven, usually between July and November. The chances of experiencing one are minimal. For a weather report, dial (407) 824-4104.

The chart below shows average maximum daytime temperatures for Orlando (the US still works on the Fahrenheit scale).

	J	F	M	A	M	J	J	A	S	O	N	D
°C	22	22	25	28	31	32	33	33	32	29	25	23
°F	71	72	78	83	88	90	91	91	89	84	77	73

CLOTHING

When it starts to get hot or sticky, Floridians turn on the air-conditioners. These can blow with an arctic chill, so don't forget to take another layer of clothing with you when shopping, dining out, or riding in air-conditioned vehicles.

Casual wear is always appropriate – something light, bright, loose, and made of cotton rather than artificial fibers. If you're likely to go swimming, bring spare swimwear for a rapid change. Other useful items include sunscreen, an umbrella or rain poncho, backpack, cap or hat, sunglasses, and comfortable walking or sports shoes.

In theme parks and on public transportation, footwear and a shirt or equivalent top cover are required.

COMPLAINTS

If something goes wrong, you'll probably be able to sort it out on the spot with the well-trained, helpful personnel typical of the service industries in Florida, and especially in the well-run theme parks. If they don't resolve your problem, ask for a supervisor or manager. Disney accommodations all have a special service telephone number to call in case of difficulties. In the theme parks, the Guest Services desks will assist you.

CRIME AND SAFETY

The big theme parks have their own security personnel, so discreet that you are hardly aware of them, but they'll be on hand if you need them. Walt Disney World Resort is among the safest environments on Earth, but you should always look after your property. Lockers are available at all theme parks. Most hotels have a safe for valuables. Never leave money, credit cards, checkbooks, cameras, etc., in a hotel room – always use the safe.

Outside the theme parks, beware of pickpockets. Car-jackings and highway crimes are not frequent, but be alert when driving. Buying and selling illegal drugs is a serious offense, and Florida has a large force of undercover police officers. If you are robbed, tell the police, and obtain a copy of the report for your insurance company. Report stolen credit cards and travelers' checks immediately. (Always keep a separate copy of the numbers. Ideally, carry a copy of your airline ticket and passport as well.)

CUSTOMS AND ENTRY REGULATIONS

British subjects and some other foreign visitors no longer require a visa to enter the US, and can instead obtain a visa waiver form from their travel agent or airline. Canadians need only evidence of their nationality. Citizens of the Republic of Ireland, Australia, New Zealand, and South Africa need a visa (but these rules can change, so consult your embassy, consulate, or travel agent). The application process can be slow, depending on individual circumstances. When you apply for a visa, bring documents which indicate when you intend to return home.

Duty-free allowance. You will be asked to fill out a customs declaration form before you arrive in the US. The following chart shows what main duty-free items you may take into the US (if you are over 21) and back into your own country.

Currency restrictions. A non-resident may take into the US free of duty and taxes, articles of up to $100 in value for use as gifts. Don't arrive with any plants, seeds, fruits, or other fresh food, as they're banned, as are liqueur chocolates. Arriving and departing passengers should report any money or checks totaling over $10,000.

Into	Cigarettes	Cigars	Tobacco	Spirits	Wine
US	200 or	50 or	2kg	1*l* or	1*l*
Australia	250 or	250g or	250g	1*l* or	1*l*
Canada	200 and	50 and	400g	1.4*l* or	1.4*l*
Ireland	200 or	50 or	250g	1*l* and	2*l*
N Zealand	200 or	50 or	250g	1.1*l* and	4.5*l*
S Africa	400 and	50 and	250g	1*l* and	2*l*
UK	200 or	50 or	250g	1*l* and	2*l*

D

DISABLED TRAVELERS

Accessibility and facilities are excellent at the theme parks and other attractions in Orlando. Special parking is available near the entrances to each park, to the hotels, and to other facilities.

Disney publishes *The Guidebook for Guests with Disabilities*. Ask at City Hall in the Magic Kingdom and at Information/Guest Services desks in other areas.

Wheelchairs are available for rent in limited numbers in several locations, usually outside or just inside the entrance. For some attractions and rides, guests may remain in wheelchairs. For others, they must be able to leave the wheelchair. Regulations are clearly indicated in leaflets and at the appropriate entrance. Some motorized wheelchairs are available for rent, and some buses and launches can accommodate conventional wheelchairs. Wheelchair access is available at toilets in all the theme parks.

For **hearing-impaired guests** a TDD (Telecommunications Device for the Deaf) is available at City Hall (Magic Kingdom Park), at Guest Services at Disney-MGM Studios and Epcot, and at Universal Studios.

Sight-impaired guests can borrow complimentary cassettes and tape recorders at the same locations. A deposit is required.

DRIVING

On the road. Drive on the right. In Florida, you may turn right after a stop at a red light, provided that there is no cross-traffic, you have given way to pedestrians, and there is no sign to the contrary. Headlights should be used when it is raining enough for windshield wipers. Seatbelts must be worn at all times, and drivers must always carry a driver's license.

Lane discipline differs from European norms. American drivers tend to stick to one lane, often making no distinction between 'fast' or 'slow' lanes. However, the left lane is generally used for passing and for going fast. You may, therefore, be overtaken on either side, so don't change lanes without careful checking.

Don't drink and drive – driving while intoxicated ('DWI') is a serious offense that could result in jail and steep fines.

Highways/expressways/motorways. Certain rules apply to high-speed divided highways (expressways). If smooth merging from the on-ramp is not possible, you must pause for an opening in traffic. A speed limit of 55mph (90km/h) operates on many highways, except on expressways in rural areas, where the limit is 65mph (105km/h).

Other speed limits, typically 30mph (48km/h) or 70km/h (45mph), apply where indicated. If you keep up with the flow of traffic, you'll have no problem. Drive any faster, and you'll be pulled over.

If you break down on an expressway, pull over to the right-hand shoulder, raise the hood (bonnet), and wait in the car for assistance with windows up and doors locked. At night, use the hazard warning lights. A cell phone is handy to have. **For emergencies, call 911.**

Tolls. Some Florida roads (including the turnpike), as well as many causeways and bridges, collect tolls. Keep a supply of coins (mostly quarters) when traveling; most toll areas provide a basket into which you drop the correct change, so there's no waiting.

Gas (petrol) and services. Florida's service stations have both self-service and full-service pumps, with fuel at the latter being more expensive. In some areas you must pre-pay, especially at night. Some pumps are operated by inserting a credit card (major international cards are accepted). Note that some stations close in the evening and on Sunday. In Walt Disney World Resort, gas stations can be found near the main entrance to the Magic Kingdom, across from Downtown Disney and near the Crossroads shopping center.

Most rental cars in Florida are equipped with air-conditioners; if your car is running low on gas or overheating, turn off the 'a/c' – it's a strain on the engine.

Parking. All the theme parks provide extensive facilities for car parking. There is usually a charge, although at Disney parks it is free if you are staying at Disney-owned accommodations and display the card that you are given when you register. If you do have to pay a parking fee, keep the ticket, since it is valid at all parks for that day. Remember to make a careful note of the exact location where you leave your car.

In general, you should park facing in the direction of traffic flow, and nose-in when angle parking is indicated (because Florida cars have no front license plates). Never park next to a fire hydrant, or a curb painted yellow or red.

Directions. Get help planning your route if you don't know the area to which you are traveling.

The American Automobile Association offers assistance to members of affiliated organizations abroad. It also provides travel information for the US and can arrange automobile insurance by the month for owner-drivers. Contact AAA at 1000 AAA Drive, Heathrow, FL 32746-5063, tel: (800) 564-6222, <www.aaasouth.com>.

Road signs. Although the US has started to use the standard international road signs, progress is gradual, and this can lead to some confusion. Detailed below are several common Anglo/American discrepancies:

American	**British**
Detour	Diversion
Divided highway	Dual carriageway
No passing	No overtaking
Railroad crossing	Level crossing
Traffic circle	Roundabout
Yield	Give way

E

ELECTRICITY

The US has 110-115 volt 60-cycle AC. Plugs are small, flat, and two- or three-pronged; foreigners will need an adapter for shavers and some other electrical appliances.

EMBASSIES AND CONSULATES

Few English-speaking countries maintain a consulate in Florida. The nearest ones to contact are listed below:

Australia: 2103 Coral Avenue, Suite 108, Miami, FL 33131, tel: (305) 858 7633.

Canada: 501 Pennsylvania Avenue, NW, Washington DC 20002, tel: (202) 682 1740.

New Zealand: Embassy, 37 Observatory Circle, NW, Washington DC 20008, tel: (202) 328 4800.
Republic of Ireland: 345 Park Avenue, 17th floor, New York, NY 10022, tel: (212) 319 2555.
South Africa: 333 East 38th Street, 9th Floor, New York, NY 10016, tel: (212) 213 4880.
United Kingdom: Brickell Bay Office Towers, Suite 2800, Miami, FL 33133, tel: (305) 374-1522.

EMERGENCIES (See also MEDICAL CARE and POLICE)

Dial **911**, and the operator will ask if you want police, ambulance, or the fire department. All towns and cities have a 24-hour number to call for medical emergencies.

First-aid posts in the Walt Disney World Resort are situated next to the Crystal Palace Restaurant, on Main Street, USA in the Magic Kingdom Park; Odyssey Center, at Future World in Epcot; the main Guest Services entrance at Disney-MGM Studios and at Creature Comforts in Safari Village at Disney's Animal Kingdom. Disney resort guests also have access to walk-in clinics. In other areas, ask for locations.

ETIQUETTE

Foreign visitors will have to get used to American informality – don't be surprised if the hotel desk clerk uses your first name.

G

GETTING TO ORLANDO

Since fares and conditions change frequently, it is advisable to consult travel agents for the latest information.

From within North America
By air. There are non-stop or direct flights every day to Orlando and other major Florida cities from most large US cities.

By bus. Florida destinations are linked to all major centers by Greyhound, the nation's major bus line, and Trailways. (New York to Orlando by express coach takes around 25 hours.) Smaller bus lines provide a comprehensive local shuttle service between hotels and attractions and also offer sightseeing tours. Be wary of long-distance, one-day tours: they don't always give sufficient time to visit. Visitors can buy unlimited Ameripasses, valid for a given length of time, to go anywhere in the country by bus at a flat rate.

By rail. Amtrak offers a variety of bargain fares; for example, children may be able to ride free, and there are tour packages with hotel and guide included. It runs a car-carrying train daily between Lorton, near Washington, DC, and Sanford, near Orlando.

By car. Travelers coming down the East Coast can take the I-95 route via Washington and Savannah. The shortest route from the West Coast is via I-10, passing Tucson, El Paso, Houston, and Mobile.

From the UK

By air. There are many non-stop and other direct flights from London Heathrow and Gatwick to Orlando and Miami. Fares include first-class, economy, excursion, APEX (Advance Purchase Excursion), business, and special 'ticket sales' and promotions available through travel agents. Generally, the longer ahead you book, the lower the fare, with the exception of standby fares, which only apply at certain times of year.

Some US airlines offer travelers from abroad a discount on the cost of each internal flight, or flat-rate unlimited-travel tickets valid for specific periods.

Charter flights and package tours. Most charter flights must be booked and paid for well in advance of the date of travel. Many package tours are available: two-center holidays divide their time between Orlando and one of the beaches (east or west coast of Florida). Other packages combine Orlando with a short cruise or a stay on a Caribbean island.

Baggage. Allowances for scheduled transatlantic flights are complex, but you are allowed to check in two suitcases of normal size. In addition, one piece of hand baggage may be carried on board. Confirm size and weight restrictions with your travel agent or air carrier when booking your ticket. It is advisable to insure all luggage for the duration of your trip.

From Elsewhere in Europe

Amsterdam has non-stop flights to Orlando, and many other European cities are linked to Florida by one-stop and other direct flights.

GUIDES AND TOURS

Some of the larger attractions provide the services of a guide. In the Magic Kingdom Park, ask at City Hall (tours begin at 9.15am); at Epcot, inquire at Guest Relations. Foreign-language guides are on call to take visitors on a quick tour that includes a selection of rides.

L

LANGUAGE

Most English-speaking foreigners are now familiar with American words and phrases. However, here are a few of the most common Anglo-American linguistic misunderstandings:

US	British
admission	entry fee
bathroom	toilet (private)
bill	banknote (money)
check/bill	bill (restaurant)
collect call	reverse charge call
elevator	lift
faucet	tap
first floor	ground floor

gas(oline)	petrol
general delivery	poste restante
liquor	spirits
liquor store	off-license
pants	trousers
pavement	road surface
purse/pocketbook	handbag
restroom	toilet (public)
second floor	first floor
sidewalk	pavement
stand in line	queue up
stroller	pushchair
subway	underground
trailer	caravan
underpass	subway
undershirt	vest
vest	waistcoat

LAUNDRY AND DRY CLEANING

Coin-operated washing machines and dryers are available at all Disney accommodations and many other hotels.

You can send laundry through most hotels from Monday to Saturday. Some laundries offer same-day service if garments are dropped off before 9am.

LOST PROPERTY

Each theme park has a Lost & Found (Lost Property) desk. At hotels, ask at the Guest Services desk or telephone Housekeeping.

Air, rail, and bus terminals and many stores have special Lost & Found areas. Restaurants put aside lost articles in the hope that someone will claim them. If your lost property is valuable, call the police. If you lose your passport, contact your consulate immediately (see pages 111–112).

M

MAPS

The free guidebook leaflets available at Guest Services/Information desks (City Hall in the Magic Kingdom, Guest Services in the main entrances of Disney-MGM Studios, Universal Studios Escape, and SeaWorld Orlando) include excellent maps.

Florida Welcome Stations on main highways and ports of entry distribute free maps, and the chamber of commerce or tourist authority will give you local maps with attractions marked on them. Service stations dispense maps from vending machines, and car rental agencies give out useful road maps.

MEDICAL CARE (See also EMERGENCIES)

Foreigners should note that the US does not provide free medical services, and that medical treatment is expensive. Arrangements should be made in advance for temporary health insurance (through a travel agent or insurance company) or ask at your local Social Security office for information on coverage during your trip.

Clinics offer less expensive access to treatment than do private practitioners. Hospital emergency rooms will treat anyone in need of speedy attention, including hospitalization in a community ward. Disney accommodations offer, for a fee, House Med, an in-room healthcare service. House Med also operates a walk-in medical clinic, at the intersection of I-4 and Highway 192.

Beware of the sun – the most common medical problem for tourists is sunburn. Start with a sunscreen with at least SPF20, or a complete-block cream at first. Build up your tan in small doses. (Sunscreen products can be bought at many area shops.) Drink plenty of water. Dehydration is another common problem: the warning signs are headaches, lassitude – and grumpy children.

Visitors from abroad will find that some medicines sold over the counter at home can be bought only by prescription in the US. There's no shortage of drugstores, or pharmacies, and a few of them are open 24 hours. Some pharmacies will deliver to hotels for a fee.

No **vaccinations** are required or recommended for Orlando.

MONEY MATTERS

Currency. The dollar is divided into 100 cents.

Banknotes: $1, $2 (rare), $5, $10, $20, $50, and $100. Larger denominations are not in general circulation. All notes are the same shape and color (except for the new $100, $50, and $20 bills, which appear slightly different from the other bills).

Coins: 1¢ (called a penny), 5¢ (nickel), 10¢ (dime), 25¢ (quarter), 50¢ (half dollar), and $1. Only the first four are commonly used. On rare occasions you may be given Canadian coins in change. They're worth about 15% less than US ones, and they don't work in automatic machines such as telephones or road toll booths.

Banks and currency exchange. Banking hours are usually 9am–5pm Monday to Friday, but very few banks change foreign currency. Walt Disney World Resort's banks are a notable exception; their hours are longer and they give a good rate of exchange. You'll find them at City Hall in the Magic Kingdom, at Guest Services windows in all parks, and at the SunTrust outlets in Town Square and across from Downtown Disney. There also are other bank branches opposite Downtown Disney and at the Crossroads of Lake Buena Vista shopping center. Large hotels also are able to change foreign money. Elsewhere it is simpler and safer to travel with travelers' checks denominated in dollars, major credit cards, or US cash.

When changing money or travelers' checks, ask for notes with a denomination of $20 or less, which are accepted everywhere.

Credit cards. When buying merchandise and tickets or paying hotel and phone bills, you will be asked 'Cash or charge?' – meaning you have the choice of paying in cash or by credit card. Businesses are wary of little-known cards, but they'll gladly accept the top American and international cards. Some international cards will work in cash dispensers if you know the PIN number, and certain banks will advance cash against the card.

Many service stations will not take money at night, only cards. Outside normal office hours, it's sometimes impossible to rent cars and pay bills with cash.

Travelers' checks are safer than cash. They can be exchanged quickly, as long as they are in US dollars. Banks usually want to see your passport or another form of identification, but many hotels, shops, and restaurants accept them directly in lieu of cash, especially those issued by American banks. Change small amounts at a time; keep the balance of your checks in your hotel safe and make a note of serial numbers and where and when you used each check.

Prices. Most displayed prices do not include the state sales tax of around 6% – it's added when you pay. The same applies to hotel bills, to which 10 or 11% is added.

The US has a larger spread of prices for the same kind of item than you might find elsewhere, as well as a greater choice. For moderately priced goods, visit the big department and discount stores. Small independent grocery stores, drugstores, and 24-hour convenience stores have price mark-ups of between 10 and 70% over the supermarkets, but independent service stations are cheaper than those of the large oil companies.

Planning Your Budget
Here's a list of average prices. They can only be broad guidelines, since inflation continues to push prices upwards.
Airport transfer: Orlando International Airport to Walt Disney World Resort: taxi $45, shuttle $15. Airport to International Drive: taxi $25, shuttle $15.
Babysitters: $5 per hour for one or two children, $1 for each additional child, plus transport expenses. Hotels, including Disney properties, charge $10 per hour.

Bicycle rental: $5 per hour, $15 per day, $35–50 per week.

Camping: Disney's Fort Wilderness offers private campgrounds. Creekside Meadow is an area exclusively for young camping. Call (407) 939 7807 for more information.

Car rental: Prices in Florida vary widely. A typical rate for a compact car, unlimited mileage, during high season might be $40 per day, $170 per week, plus insurance.

Entertainment: Cinema $4.50–10; nightclub/disco $5–20, including cover charge; drinks $4–10; dinner and show $30–60.

Hotels (double room with bathroom): Walt Disney World Resort: deluxe $250 and up, standard $150, moderate $75. Elsewhere: deluxe $150 and up, moderate $70–100, budget $40–80, motel $30–50.

Laundry: Shirt $1.50, blouse $2.50. Dry cleaning: jacket $5 and up, trousers $4, dress $9.

Meals and drinks: Continental breakfast $2–10, full breakfast $5–15, lunch in snack bar $5, in restaurant $10–15, dinner $15–40 (more with entertainment), coffee $1.50, beer $2–3, glass of wine $3–6, carafe of wine $6–10, bottle of wine $9–25, cocktail $4–6.50.

Petrol/gas: $2 and up per U.S. gallon (approximately 4 liters).

Taxi (Orlando area): $3 for first mile, plus $2 per following mile.

N

NEWSPAPERS AND MAGAZINES

Local newspapers and the national daily USA Today are sold in drugstores, grocery stores and from vending machines. Special newsstands carry *The New York Times*, *The Wall Street Journal*, and *The Miami Herald*, as well as a variety of other newspapers. *The Orlando Sentinel* provides information about central Florida and gives TV programs, opening hours of attractions, pages of grocery store bargains, and coupons for price reductions at various restaurants. Newspapers and magazines from Britain, Germany, France, Italy, etc, are usually available the day following publication in larger stores and hotels.

O

OPENING HOURS

Three Disney theme parks open at 9am officially, but that applies to the rides and other attractions; the **Magic Kingdom's Main Street, U.S.A.** is open at 8am and the gates at **Epcot** and **Disney-MGM Studios** open at 8.30am. **Disney's Animal Kingdom** opens at 8am. Closing hours vary widely from park to park, day to day, and season to season. Check with Disney hotels or Disney information (407) 824 4321 for details.

In the parks, **breakfast and snack places** keep the same hours as the parks: beware that some restaurants may not open until 11am. Elsewhere, breakfast is served from 6 or 7am, lunch from 11am, and dinner from as early as 5pm until 10 or 11pm.

Business hours are from 8 or 8.30am to 5 or 5.30pm. Shops open from 9 or 10am. Closing hours vary from 5.30 to 9pm (and some supermarkets and convenience stores are open round the clock).

Blizzard Beach and **Typhoon Lagoon**: usually open at 10am and close by 5pm, with extended summertime hours.

Pleasure Island: clubs and entertainment open at 7pm and close at 2am (the shops are open from 10am).

SeaWorld Orlando: open from 9am to 6–10pm depending on the time of year.

Universal Orlando Resort: open from 9am; closing time varies.

P

PETS

Pets may not be taken into the theme parks, which operate kennels for pets near the entrance to each park.

In many places, dogs are not allowed to run free, and they are usually barred from beaches, hotels, restaurants, food shops, and public transportation.

PHOTOGRAPHY AND VIDEO

Camera shops sell film, but drugstores and supermarkets supply the same at discount prices. A two-hour printing service is available in major theme parks and elsewhere. Don't store film in the car; it could be damaged in the intense heat from the sun. Airport security X-ray machines are safe for normal film, whether exposed or unused. Super-fast film may be affected. Ask for separate inspection.

You can rent cameras and video cameras for use on Disney property at photographic shops. Videotape is available for all types of cameras. Pre-recorded tapes bought in the US will not function on European systems and vice versa; nor will the tapes you make on rented equipment, and conversion is expensive.

POLICE (See also EMERGENCIES)

City police are concerned with local crime and traffic violations, while Florida Highway Patrol officers (also called State Troopers) ensure highway safety and are on the lookout for people speeding or driving under the influence of alcohol or drugs. Walt Disney World Resort has its own security force and road patrol. American police officers are generally friendly and tolerant of mild transgressions by foreigners. **For emergencies, dial 911** (fire, police, ambulance).

POST OFFICES

The US postal service deals mainly with mail. Telephone and telegraph services are operated by other companies. Post your letters in the blue curbside boxes. The buff-colored ones in Main Street, U.S.A., are cleared by Disney personnel and the letters taken to a post office. You can buy stamps from City Hall in the Magic Kingdom, and from machines in post office entrance halls after hours (there's also a post office at the Crossroads at Lake Buena Vista shopping center).
Post office hours are from 8am to 4.30 or 5pm, Monday–Friday, and 8am–noon on Saturday.

General Delivery (Poste restante). You can have mail marked 'General Delivery' sent to you care of the main post office of any town. The letters will be held for one month.

Take your passport or some other form of ID with you when you go to collect it.

PUBLIC HOLIDAYS

If a holiday, such as Christmas Day, falls on a Sunday, banks and most stores close on the following day.

New Year's Day	1 January
*Martin Luther King Jr. Day**	Third Monday in January
*President's Day**	Third Monday in February
Memorial Day	Last Monday in May
Independence Day	4 July
Labor Day	First Monday in September
*Columbus Day**	Second Monday in October
*Veterans' Day**	11 November
*Election Day**	November (moveable)
Thanksgiving	Fourth Thursday in November
Christmas Day	25 December

* Most shops and businesses open

R

RADIO AND TV

Numerous AM and FM radio stations broadcast pop, rock, 'urban,' and country-and-western music, but each city has at least one classical station.

Every hotel room has a television carrying many channels, some are 24-hour.

Florida news begins around 6pm (national and international news at 6.30 or 7pm), and is broadcast on several networks. Many hotels carry CNN, which broadcasts news around the clock.

RELIGION

There are Catholic services at Disney's Polynesian Resort (Sundays at 8 and 10.15am) and a Protestant service here at 9am. Elsewhere, Saturday newspapers often list church service schedules for the following day. Besides Catholic, Episcopalian, Presbyterian, and Methodist churches, you'll see branches of fundamentalist and Southern Baptist denominations. Jewish services are held at the synagogues in Orlando. Muslim prayer services take place at Jama Masjid (tel: (407) 238 2700).

S

SMOKING

Smoking is not permitted on any attraction, ride, or in any waiting area in theme parks. All Disney restaurants are smoke-free. Other restaurants in town have taken that lead, though many eateries have designated smoking and non-smoking areas – mention your preference before being seated. Non-smoking rooms are available at most hotels – ask when making your reservation or when you check in.

T

TELEPHONES

American telephone companies are efficient and reliable. Phones are found in the streets, at service stations, and in shopping plazas, restaurants, and most public buildings. Directions explaining how to use them are posted on the instrument. To make a local call, lift the receiver, put 35¢ in the slot, wait for the tone, then enter the 10-digit number. The operator will automatically inform you of any additional charge, so have some change ready.

For **local directory inquiries** enter 411. For local operator assistance and for help within the same area code, enter 0. For directory assistance in another area, enter 1, then area code, then 555 1212.

Long-distance calls may be dialed direct from a pay phone if you follow the directions. The prefix 1 is usually needed. If you don't know
the correct area code, enter 00 for assistance. Long-distance calls cost
more from a pay-phone than from a private one.

The international access code is 011, followed by the country code.

Charges are listed in the introduction to the white pages of the telephone directory, with information on person-to-person (personal), collect (reverse-charge) and credit card calls. Some companies no longer
accept major credit cards. Numbers with an 800, 877, or 888 prefix
are toll-free, although some hotels add a charge when you call out.
They may also begin charging after a certain number of 'rings' even
though there has been no answer, so don't hold on too long.

Faxes can be sent from larger hotels and from office service bureaus
in some shopping malls.

TIME DIFFERENCES

The US (mainland) has four time zones; Florida (like New York) is
on Eastern Standard Time (EST). Between April and October Day-
light Saving Time is adopted and clocks move ahead one hour. The
chart below shows the time in other cities in winter at noon in Florida:

Los Angeles	Orlando	London	Sydney
9am	noon	5pm	4am
Sunday	Sunday	Sunday	Monday

Dates in the US often are written differently from the European
day/month/year system; for example, 1/17/06 means 17 January 2006.

TIPPING

In many restaurants waiters and waitresses earn most of their salary
from tips; often they are paid little else. Cinema or theater ushers and
gas station attendants are not tipped. Some suggestions:

Tour guide	10–15%
Hairdresser/barber	15%
Hotel porter	50¢–$1, per bag (minimum $1)

Taxi driver	15%
Waiter	15–20%

TOILETS/RESTROOMS

Theme parks have many public toilets marked 'restrooms.' Elsewhere you can find them in restaurants, railway stations, and large stores.

TOURIST INFORMATION (See also WEBSITES)

For information prior to arrival, contact one of the following: Orlando Tourism Bureau, Russell Chambers, The Piazza, Covent Garden, London, WC2E 8AA, tel: (020) 7233 2305; Florida Division of Tourism in Europe, Brochure line: (01737) 644 882, <www.visitflorida.com>; The Walt Disney Company (UK), tel: (020) 8222 2846; Walt Disney World, Box 10,000, Lake Buena Vista, FL 32830-1000, USA, tel: (407) 824 4321, <www.disneyworld.com>.

In Disney hotels, TV channels 5, 7, and 10 give information, and you can telephone (407) 824 4321 for yet more information.

TRANSPORTATION (See also AIRPORTS, CAR RENTAL, DRIVING, and GETTING TO ORLANDO)

The Walt Disney World Resort transportation system is complex, as are the rules about who can use it. They include those staying in Disney accommodation, at the Plaza hotels, or those carrying four- or five-day passes. Additionally, those with Magic Kingdom tickets can use the monorail or ferry to get to its entrance.

Disney buses connect all areas within the Walt Disney World Resort. They carry color codes and prominent signs.

The **Disney World Monorail** links Disney's Magic Kingdom resorts with the Magic Kingdom Park and Epcot.

Ferries operate between the TTC and the Magic Kingdom Park entrance; between the Contemporary Resort and Magic Kingdom Park; and between the Walt Disney World Swan, Walt Disney World

Dolphin, and Yacht and Beach Club resorts, Board Walk Inn, and Disney-MGM Studios.

Taxis always carry a roof sign. Most taxis have meters, and the rates are generally painted on the doors. A few taxis wait at theme parks and other attractions toward closing time. Otherwise, you will have to telephone and request a car (consult Yellow Pages under Taxicabs).

W

WEBSITES

For information about Walt Disney World Resort and details of Disney accommodations, go to <www.disneyworld.com>. The Orlando/Orange County Convention & Visitors Bureau <www.orlandoinfo.com> provides information on lodging, dining, attractions, and transportation. At <www.orlandotouristinformationbureau.com>, you'll find general travel information. For good deals on lodging and transportation, try <www.go2orlando.com>. Other websites include:

Kennedy Space Center <www.kennedyspacecenter.com>
SeaWorld Orlando <www.seaworld.com>
Universal Orlando Resort <www.universalstudios.com>.

WEIGHTS AND MEASURES (See also Driving)

The United States is one of the last countries in the world to change officially from the imperial to the metric system.

Y

YOUTH HOSTELS

The US is not well endowed with youth hostels, although some budget hotels make rooms available to International YHA members at a large discount. There is no age limit. For further information, write to the American Youth Hostels, 733 15th Street, Suite 840, Washington, DC 20005, tel: (202) 783 6161, <www.hiayh.org>.

Recommended Hotels

The Orlando area, including Walt Disney World Resort, has more hotel rooms than any US metropolitan area except Las Vegas. Fierce competition means that you'll be assured of value for money, whether you choose a luxury resort, a modest motel or something in between.

This selection of hotels in each price range is listed alphabetically. Location is important and should hinge on whether your plans are to spend most of your time at Disney and other nearby attractions or to travel more widely in central Florida. To help, the accommodations list is sub-divided by area and each entry marked with a symbol indicating the price range, per night, for a double room with bath, excluding breakfast. Taxes of about 10% are added to hotel bills.

In the US, rates are quoted for the room, not per person. If you have more than two occupants, there may be a small additional charge. Some hotels include a simple Continental breakfast. Always ask about special-rate packages for stays of more than one day. All hotels listed here accept major credit cards.

$$$$	above $220
$$$	$120–$220
$$	$80–$120
$	below $80

WALT DISNEY WORLD RESORT

Guests staying in themed Disney accommodations may use Disney transportation and recreation facilities and receive preferential treatment for dining and show reservations. Car parking at the theme parks is free for guests of Disney accommodations, and entry to parks via Disney transportation is nearly always guaranteed, even when park attendance is high. These advantages, as well as the detailed theming and proximity of accommodations to Disney's parks, compensate for some higher room prices within Walt Disney World Resort. *All Disney accommodations can be booked on the internet at www.disneyworld.com or at the central reservation number: (407) 934 7639.*

Disney's All-Star Resorts $$ *Walt Disney World Resort, Lake Buena Vista, FL 32830, tel: (407) W-DISNEY [934 7639].* Sprawling sports-, music- and movie-themed resort, featuring whimsical icons outside, several pools, food court, and nicely decorated rooms. Disney's most inexpensive accommodation, located near Disney's Animal Kingdom. Wheelchair access. 5,760 rooms.

Disney's Animal Kingdom Lodge $$$ *Walt Disney World Resort, Lake Buena Vista, FL 32830, tel: (407) 938 3000.* Wake up to giraffes and zebras – most rooms have balconies overlooking either the Savannah or Pool. The thatched roofs and tent-like rooms are safari-style and hearty African food is served in two restaurants, Jiko and Boma, which has an open-air kitchen. 1,293 rooms.

Disney's BoardWalk Inn & Villas $$$$ *Walt Disney World Resort, Lake Buena Vista, FL 32830, tel: (407) 939 5100.* Re-creating the grand boardwalk beach resorts of the mid-20th century, the 378-room BoardWalk Inn and 517-unit BoardWalk Villas offer deluxe rooms or large suites for families. Near Epcot and Disney-MGM Studios, with shopping, dining, and convention center on site. Wheelchair access. 910 rooms.

Disney's Caribbean Beach Resort $$$ *Walt Disney World Resort, Lake Buena Vista, FL 32830, tel: (407) 934 3400.* Near Epcot and Disney-MGM Studios, this Caribbean-themed 'village' sits beachfront along a lake and has a themed recreation area, marina, shopping, and food-court dining. Wheelchair access. 2,112 rooms.

Disney's Contemporary Resort $$$$ *Walt Disney World Resort, Lake Buena Vista, FL 32830, tel: (407) 824 1000.* This 15-story resort overlooks the Magic Kingdom. Monorail service passes through the massive fourth-floor concourse. Best restaurant in town – California Grill – offers a panoramic view from the top floor. Marina, parasailing, convention center, and child care. Wheelchair access. 1,041 rooms and suites.

Disney's Coronado Springs Resort $$$ *Walt Disney World Resort, Lake Buena Vista, FL 32830, tel: (407) 939 1000.* The American Southwest and Mexico come alive in this hacienda-style resort set on a large lake. An imposing Mayan pyramid pool area, full service Mexican dining and food court, convention center. Parking near each group of rooms. Wheelchair access. 1,967 rooms.

Disney's Grand Floridian Resort & Spa $$$$ *Walt Disney World Resort, Lake Buena Vista, FL 32830, tel: (407) 824 3000.* A masterfully re-created Victorian hotel, the Grand Floridian is the most elegant of Disney accommodations. Deluxe spa and health club, monorail service, several first-rate restaurants, high tea, marina, beach, child care. Wheelchair access. 900 rooms and suites.

Disney's Old Key West Resort $$$$ *Walt Disney World Resort, Lake Buena Vista, FL 32830, tel: (407) 827 7700.* A vacation home resort with deluxe studios or one-, two-, and three- bedroom villas with full kitchen and whirlpool bathtubs. Health club, sauna, pool, recreational activities. Wheelchair access. 709 villas.

Disney's Polynesian Resort $$$$ *Walt Disney World Resort, Lake Buena Vista, FL 32830, tel: (407) 824 2000.* A South Pacific mood is evoked in this resort next to the Seven Seas Lagoon. Monorail service, beach, restaurants, dinner show, child care. Wheelchair access. 853 rooms and suites.

Disney's Port Orleans French Quarter $$$ *Walt Disney World Resort, Lake Buena Vista, FL 32830, tel: (407) 934 5000.* Near Epcot, this moderate hotel is reminiscent of New Orleans. Parking is close to rooms. Riverboat rides to Downtown Disney, full-service dining, food court, child-friendly pool. 1,008 rooms.

Disney's Port Orleans-Riverside $$$ *Walt Disney World Resort, Lake Buena Vista, FL 32830, tel: (407) 934 6000.* Close to Epcot, this hotel is surrounded by a wooded setting, and features an Old South theme with plantation homes. Old-fashioned swimming hole with slides and rope swings, riverboat transportation to Downtown Disney. Wheelchair access. 2,048 rooms.

Disney's Wilderness Lodge $$$ *Walt Disney World Resort, Lake Buena Vista, FL 32830, tel: (407) 824 3200.* Perched on the shore of Bay Lake and surrounded by woods, this faux-rustic lodge is styled complete with totem poles in a Western motif and has one of Disney's finest hotel lobbies. A geothermal 'geyser' erupts hourly from a rocky outcrop. Boat and bus service to parks, full-service dining, hot- and cold-spa, pool, child care. Wheelchair access. 728 rooms.

Disney's Yacht & Beach Club Resorts $$$$ *Walt Disney World Resort, Lake Buena Vista, FL 32830, tel: (407) 934 7000/8000.* A short stroll or boat ride to Epcot's International Gateway. Hotels are themed to a 19th-century coastal Massachusetts resort. Dining variety, convention center, child care, marina, elaborate pools, sand-bottom lagoon, and beach. Wheelchair access. 1,213 rooms and suites.

AFFILIATED HOTELS OF WALT DISNEY WORLD RESORT

Several fine hotels not owned by Disney are also located on Disney grounds. Entry to theme parks by Disney bus is guaranteed, and many Disney amenities are included.

Internet booking is available for these resorts through the main website, <www.disneyworld.com>.

Best Western Lake Buena Vista Resort $$$ *2000 Hotel Plaza Boulevard, Lake Buena Vista, FL; 32830, tel: (800) 348 3765.* Caribbean-style resort with 18th-floor nightclub overlooking Disney, plus swimming, playground, and shopping. Wheelchair access. 325 rooms.

Courtyard by Marriott $$$ *1805 Hotel Plaza Boulevard, Lake Buena Vista, FL 32830, tel: (800) 223 9930.* Includes 14-story tower and lower annex. Pools, garden, and family-oriented dining, all in walking distance to Downtown Disney. 323 rooms.

Grosvenor Resort $$$ *1850 Hotel Plaza Boulevard, Lake Buena Vista, FL 32830, tel: (407) 828 4444.* Lakeside resort with convention facilities. Recreational facilities, restaurants and meeting space. Wheelchair access. 620 rooms.

Hilton $$$$ *1751 Hotel Plaza Boulevard, Lake Buena Vista, FL 32830, tel: (407) 827 4000.* Resort located across from Downtown Disney with convention center, recreation, pools, nine restaurants, and child care. Wheelchair access. 814 rooms.

Hotel Royal Plaza $$$ *1905 Hotel Plaza Boulevard, Lake Buena Vista, FL 32830, tel: (800) 248 7890.* Close to Downtown Disney, this 17-story hotel features dining, entertainment, recreation, and meeting space. Wheelchair access. 394 rooms.

Walt Disney World Dolphin $$$$ *Operated by Sheraton Hotels, 1500 Epcot Resorts Boulevard, Lake Buena Vista, FL 32830-2653, tel: (800) 934 4000.* Close to Epcot's International Gateway, this resort is a study in whimsy crowned by giant dolphin icons. Marina, health club, child care. Wheelchair access. 1,510 rooms and suites.

Walt Disney World Swan $$$$ *Operated by Westin Hotels, 1200 Epcot Resorts Boulevard, Lake Buena Vista, FL 32830-2786, tel: (407) 934 3000.* Sister hotel to the Dolphin, the Swan features graceful swan icons, and same amenities. Wheelchair access. 758 rooms and suites. Both resorts were designed by the renowned architect Michael Graves.

Wyndham Palace Resort & Spa $$$ *1900 Buena Vista Drive, Lake Buena Vista, FL 32830, tel: (407) 827 2727 or (800) 996-3426.* A lakeside, 27-story tower complex. Convention center, recreation facilities, award-winning Arthur's 27 fine-dining restaurant. Wheelchair access. 1,013 rooms and suites.

CLOSE TO WALT DISNEY WORLD RESORT/KISSIMMEE

Days Inn Maingate East $$ *52840 West Irlo Bronson Memorial Highway (US 192), Kissimmee, FL 34746, tel: (407) 396 7969 or (800) 327 9126.* Budget hotel with pools. Close to the Magic Kingdom. Wheelchair access. 604 rooms.

Holiday Inn Hotel & Suites Maingate East $$ *5678 West Irlo Bronson Memorial Highway (US 192), Kissimmee, FL 34746, tel: (407) 396 4488 or (800) 366 5437.* Large family-oriented hotel near the Magic Kingdom, pools, children's entertainment, and special 'kid suites' for children. Wheelchair access. 614 rooms and suites.

Howard Johnson Inn Maingate East $ *6051 West Irlo Bronson Memorial Highway. (US 192), Kissimmee, FL 34747, tel: (407) 396 1748 or (800) 288 4678.* Motel with pool near the Magic Kingdom. Children under 12 eat meals at no charge. Wheelchair access. 567 good-sized rooms.

Hyatt Regency Grand Cypress Resort $$$$ *One Grand Cypress Boulevard, Orlando, FL 32836, tel: (407) 239 1234 or (800) 55HYATT [554 9288].* A luxurious resort in a lush garden setting near Downtown Disney. Golf, racquet club, windsurfing on the lake, 'Kid's Club,' and equestrian center. 750 rooms and suites.

Larson's Inn Family Suites $ *6075 West Irlo Bronson Memorial Highway (US 192), Kissimmee, FL 34747, tel: (407) 396 6100.* Budget hotel with pool and hot tub. Not far from the Magic Kingdom. Wheelchair access. 120 rooms and suites.

Marriott Orlando World Center $$$$ *8701 World Center Drive, Orlando, FL 32821, tel: (407) 239 4200.* A towering resort hotel near Disney complete with convention center, golf, tennis, pools, and gardens. Wheelchair access. 1,500 rooms.

Orange Lake Resort & Country Club $$ *8505 West Irlo Bronson Memorial Highway (US 192), Kissimmee, FL 34747, tel: (407) 239 0000.* A lakeside resort complex of villas near the Magic Kingdom. Water sports, tennis, pools, golf course. Wheelchair access. 1,344 studio villas and 1-, 2-, and 3-bedroom villas.

Ramada Resort Maingate $$ *2950 Reedy Creek Boulevard, Kissimmee, FL 34747, tel: (407) 396 4466 or (800) ENJOYFL [365 6935].* Comfortable, family-oriented lodgings near the Magic Kingdom. Pools and tennis. Wheelchair access. 278 rooms.

UNIVERSAL HOTELS

Hard Rock Hotel $$$–$$$$ *800 Universal Boulevard, Orlando, FL 32819, tel: (407) 503-7625.* Rock 'n' roll memorabilia is the theme at this luxurious hotel. Accommodations range from standard rooms to opulent suites. Palm-shaded pool with a beach, and outdoor bar. Several lounges and restaurants. 650 rooms and suites.

Portofino Bay Hotel $$$–$$$$$ *5601 Universal Boulevard, Orlando, FL 32819, tel: (407) 503-1000.* Universal's most luxurious accommodations are housed in this re-creation of Portofino, Italy. Facilities include elaborate pools, spa, restaurants and lounges. Gourmet dining at the Delfino Riviera. 750 rooms and suites.

Royal Pacific Resort $$–$$$$ *6300 Hollywood Way, Orlando, FL 32819, tel: (407) 503-3000.* Centered on a lagoon-like pool surrounded by cabanas, palm trees, a beach, and a waterfall, Universal's 'budget' hotel is inspired by the South Pacific. Rooms are more modestly furnished and smaller than those at other on-site hotels. Five restaurants, including the Tchoup Chop, an Asian eatery run by celebrity chef Emeril Lagasse.

ORLANDO: INTERNATIONAL DRIVE AREA

Fairfield Inn by Marriott $ *8342 Jamaican Court, Orlando, FL 32819, tel: (407) 363 1944.* Cozy economy hotel with continental breakfast included in the room rate. Close to SeaWorld. Wheelchair access. 134 rooms.

Holiday Inn Express $$ *6323 International Drive, Orlando, FL 32819, tel: (407) 351 4430 or (800) 365 6935.* Hotel located across from Wet 'n' Wild water park. Some rooms feature microwave oven and refrigerator. Wheelchair access. 218 rooms.

Howard Johnson Universal Gateway Inn $ *7050 Kirkman Road, Orlando, FL 32819, tel: (407) 351 2000 or (800) 327 3808.* Family-oriented economy hotel featuring two pools, located near Universal Studios Escape. Wheelchair access. 354 rooms.

The Peabody Orlando $$$$ *9801 International Drive, Orlando, FL 32819, tel: (407) 352 4000 or (800) PEABODY [732-2639].* A 27-story landmark hotel in the tourist corridor complete with Olympic-sized swimming pool and convention center. Known for its twice-daily 'March of the Peabody Ducks' and weekday high tea. 891 rooms.

Renaissance Orlando Resort $$$ *6677 Sea Harbor Drive, Orlando, FL 32821, tel: (407) 351 5555.* Ten-story tower and convention complex well suited to families. Located across from Sea-World, with Olympic-sized pool and tennis courts. Wheelchair access. 780 rooms.

Sheraton Studio City Resort $$ *5905 International Drive, Orlando, FL; 32819, tel: (407) 351 2100.* An economical, 21-story round hotel evoking Hollywood of the 1940s and '50s, located across from Universal Studios Escape. Pools. Wheelchair access. 302 deluxe rooms.

Sheraton World Resort $$ *10100 International Drive, Orlando, FL 32821, tel: (407) 352 1100.* Low-rise buildings surrounded by gardens and located near SeaWorld. Three swimming pools, mini-golf, refrigerator and coffee maker in each room. Wheelchair access. 789 rooms.

ORLANDO: NORTH AND DOWNTOWN

Orlando Marriott Downtown $$$ *400 West Livingston Street, Orlando, FL 32801, tel: (407) 843 6664.* A 15-story downtown hotel across from the Orlando Arena and the Car Performing Arts Centre. Casual dining and signature sports bar. Wheelchair access. 290 rooms.

The Westin Grand Bohemian $$$$ *325 South Orange Avenue, Orlando, FL 32801 (407) 313 9000.* This award-winning, AAA four-diamond hotel in Secessionist style calls itself 'an experience in art and music'. Try a martini in the Bösendorfer Lounge. 250 rooms including 36 suites.

Recommended Restaurants

The Greater Orlando area has more than 4,000 dining and drinking establishments, and many of the restaurants serve first-rate fare. Most eateries are open seven days a week. Here is a selection of full-service restaurants, buffet restaurants, and food courts (multiple outlets sharing a table area); our space will not allow listing even a fraction of the vast number of quick-service restaurants and all-you-can-eat buffets that are well within our lowest price range. Many restaurants outside the theme parks serve inexpensive lunch buffets, then offer full-service dining in the evening. Entries are listed in alphabetical order with a symbol indicating the per-person price range for a three-course meal. Drinks, gratuities and 6% sales tax are not included. All restaurants listed here accept major credit cards.

$$$	$30 and over
$$	$15–$30
$	up to $15

WALT DISNEY WORLD RESORT

Most full-service Disney restaurants will book priority seating for guests who call (407) WDW-DINE [939 3463].

Akershus $$ *Norway Pavilion, Epcot (priority seating).* Norwegian buffet of cold and hot dishes, from herring and salmon to goat's cheese and desserts.

Artist Point $$$ *Wilderness Lodge (priority seating).* Fresh salmon roasted on cedar planks plus wild game options make this a truly fine dining experience.

Biergarten $$ *Germany Pavilion, Epcot (priority seating).* Hearty buffet includes veal, *spaetzle*, *bratwurst*, and other German specialties, with traditional Bavarian entertainment by musicians, dancers, and yodelers.

Bongos Cuban Cafe $$ *Downtown Disney West Side*. Cuban cuisine in a restaurant owned by Gloria Estefan and her husband, Emilio, and showcasing the tastes of Miami and South Beach.

California Grill $$$ *Contemporary Resort (priority seating)*. West Coast cuisine including wood-oven pizza, pan-seared tuna, and all market-fresh ingredients. Excellent *sushi* and vegetarian dishes. Breathtaking 15th-floor view of the Magic Kingdom.

Cape May Café $$ *Beach Club Resort (priority seating)*. All-you-can-eat. New England-style clambake every night. Seafood buffets.

Cap'n Jack's Oyster Bar $$ *Downtown Disney Marketplace*. Pier house restaurant featuring crab, lobster, clams, and oysters, plus 'land lubber' specials.

Le Cellier Steakhouse $$ *Canada Pavilion, Epcot (priority seating)*. Maple-glazed salmon, prime rib, Canadian specialties, and beers.

Chef Mickey's $$ *Contemporary Resort (priority seating)*. Family-friendly buffet of pasta, seafood, and standard American fare. Seasonal offerings and sundae bar. 'Chef' Mickey Mouse appears at character breakfasts and during evening meals.

Les Chefs de France $$$ *France Pavilion (priority seating)*. Exceptional service and innovative cuisine, including specialties by chefs Paul Bocuse and Roger Vergé, as well as master pastry chef Gaston Lenôtre.

Cinderella's Royal Table $$ *Cinderella Castle, Magic Kingdom Park (priority seating)*. Festive medieval setting serves up Once Upon A Time character breakfast. Salads and sandwiches at midday. Dinner menu includes spice-crusted salmon and beef tenderloin.

Citricos $$$ *Grand Floridian Resort & Spa (priority seating)*. Seasonal Florida cuisine with Mediterranean flair such as grilled tiger shrimp with sweet potato puree and fig compote.

Coral Reef $$$ *The Living Seas Pavilion, Epcot (priority seating)*. Enjoys a panoramic view of artificial reef. The menu features seafood bisques and grills, fresh fish, and pasta selections.

Dolphin Fountain $ *Walt Disney World Dolphin, tel: (407) 934 4000*. A 1950s-style ice-cream parlor with burgers, shakes, fries, and lots of ice-cream, of course.

End Zone $ *All-Star Sports Resorts*. Sports-themed food court featuring all-time favorites such as pizza, pastas, chicken, ribs, sandwiches, and frozen yogurt.

50s Prime Time Café $$ *Disney-MGM Studios (priority seating)*. Watch black-and-white TV playing 1950s sitcoms and eat favorites from the era such as meatloaf, french fries with chili and cheese, fried chicken, and pot roast. Thick milk shakes, apple pie, and banana splits for dessert.

Flying Fish Cafe $$$ *Disney's BoardWalk (priority seating)*. One of Disney's best in a whimsical setting with busy stage kitchen. Potato-wrapped yellowtail snapper and other creative dishes.

Garden Grill $$ *The Land Pavilion, Epcot (priority seating)*. Revolving restaurant overlooking scenic murals and boat ride. Salads and vegetables are home-grown in The Land greenhouses. Full country breakfast stars Mickey, Minnie, Chip, and Dale.

Garden Grove Cafe $$ *Walt Disney World Swan, tel: (407) 934 1609*. Spacious, five-story greenhouse eatery serves full breakfast menu, fresh fish at lunch, and continental fare in the evening.

Hollywood Brown Derby $$ *Disney-MGM Studios (priority seating)*. Home of famous Cobb salad, the Derby serves up fresh fish, pasta, and steaks in 1930s California-revisited atmosphere.

House of Blues $$ *Downtown Disney West Side*. Live music every night. Southern specialties include jambalaya, etouffee, seafood gumbo, and bread pudding.

Liberty Tree Tavern $$ *Liberty Square, Magic Kingdom (priority seating)*. Decorated in the style of an 18th-century inn. Cooking has a New England touch with stews, chowders, fresh fish, and bread bowls. All-you-can-eat dinner feast includes roast turkey and honey mustard ham.

L'Originale Alfredo di Roma Ristorante $$$ *Italy Pavilion, Epcot (priority seating)*. Colorful, festive offshoot of the famous Roman restaurant. Specialty is *fettuccine Alfredo*. All pastas are made fresh. Strolling musicians entertain guests.

Marrakesh $$$ *Morocco Pavilion, Epcot (priority seating)*. Moroccan specialties and sampler platters: couscous, kebabs, and roast lamb. Meals served to the accompaniment of musicians and a belly dancer.

Mitsukoshi $$$ *Japan Pavilion, Epcot (priority seating)*. *Sushi*, *tempura*, and stir-fry reign at this complex of Japanese eateries. At the Teppanyaki Dining Room, chefs entertain with their cooking. Martinis made with *sake*.

Narcoossee's $$$ *Grand Floridian Resort & Spa (priority seating)*. Sweeping lakeside setting for dinner only. Inventive cuisine uses fresh ingredients. Soft-shell crabs and Prince Edward Island mussels in white wine and garlic are signature dishes.

Old Port Royale $ *Caribbean Beach Resort*. Food court with six counters offering roasts, burgers, soups, and salads.

Palio $$$ *Walt Disney World Swan, tel: (407) 934 1281*. Northern Italian cooking in an elegant setting. Strolling musicians accompany the meal.

Planet Hollywood $$ *Downtown Disney, tel: (407) 827 7827*. Movie memorabilia cram every inch of this zany blue sphere, part of the international chain launched by Arnold Schwarzenegger, Bruce Willis, Sly Stallone, and entrepreneur Robert Earl. Hefty platters of burgers, sandwiches, steaks, and pasta.

Portobello Yacht Club $$ *Pleasure Island, tel: (407) 934 8888*. First-rate Northern Italian cuisine and seafood specialties.

Rainforest Café $$ *Downtown Disney Marketplace*. Eat in the midst of volcanoes, simulated rainstorms, and a colorful troop of rainforest animals. Pasta, sandwiches, salads, ribs, and other American specialties.

Rose & Crown $$ *UK Pavilion, Epcot (priority seating)*. Traditional British fare: roast beef and Yorkshire pudding, fish and chips, trifle, and cheeses in a polished dining room or outdoors beneath umbrellas.

San Angel Inn $$ *Mexico Pavilion, Epcot (priority seating)*. Mexican dishes ranging from the familiar to the unusual in a scenic indoor setting. Try the *mole poblano* (chicken with spices and chocolate).

Sci-Fi Dine-In Theater $$ *Disney-MGM Studios (priority seating)*. Sit in mock-ups of 1950s convertibles and watch clips from old sci-fi films as you dine on sandwiches, salads, and tempting desserts.

Spoodles $$–$$$ *BoardWalk (priority seating)*. Mediterranean specialties, including Moroccan spiced tuna, grilled lamb chops, and wood-fired flat breads. Appetizing *tapas* menu. One of Disney's best breakfast buffets.

Tusker House $ *Disney's Animal Kingdom*. A great counter-service dining experience with fried chicken in African spices, roasted vegetables on *foccacia* bread, and other unusual choices.

Wolfgang Puck Cafe $–$$$ *Downtown Disney (priority seating for upstairs dining room)*. West Coast creations featuring Puck's famous pizza, Thai specialties, *sushi*, and magnificent salads. The downstairs cafe is less expensive and the food just as tasty.

ELSEWHERE IN THE ORLANDO AREA

Arthur's 27 $$$ *Wyndham Palace Resort, 1900 Lake Buena Vista Drive, tel: (407) 827 3450*. The food is just slightly less spectacular than the view at this elegant, 27th-floor restaurant, featuring expertly prepared Continental cuisine. Ask to be seated in time for the fireworks at Disney World. Reservations required.

Bahama Breeze $$ *8849 International Drive, Orlando, tel: (407) 248 2499.* A taste of the Caribbean, from the coconut shrimp and paella to the piña colada bread pudding for dessert. Listen to the live band while you wait.

Boheme Restaurant $$$ *325 South Orange Avenue, tel: (407) 313 9000.* A sumptuous art-filled dining room in the Westin Grand Bohemian Hotel sets the stage for sophisticated Continental dishes. Highlights include jumbo 'peeky toe' crab cake, asparagus-crusted scallops, and pepper-seared Angus carpaccio. Sunday jazz brunch.

El Bohio Cafe $ *5756 Dahlia Drive, Orlando, tel: (407) 282 1723.* Some of the best authentic Cuban cuisine in the area, including sweet fried plantains, flan, and stuffed yuca. *Ropa vieja* is a traditional favorite.

Bubbalou's Bodacious Bar-B-Q $ *1471 Lee Road, Winter Park, tel: (407) 423 1212.* Small, southern-style barbecue spot with very casual atmosphere and first-rate ribs.

Cafe Tu-Tu Tango $-$$ *8625 International Drive, Orlando, tel: (407) 248 2222.* Serves wide variety of *tapas* – small appetizer dishes. Artists and performers roam the restaurant.

Capriccio Grill $$$ *Peabody Hotel, 9801 International Drive, Orlando, tel: (407) 352 4450.* Authentic Italian country cooking with top-quality fresh ingredients.

Cariera's Cucina Italiana $ *Marketplace Shopping Center, 7600 Dr. Phillips Boulevard., Orlando, tel: (407) 351 1187.* Pizza, *fettucini* and other Italian specialities.

Columbia $ *649 Front Street, Celebration, tel: (407) 566 1505.* Housed in what looks like an old Spanish palace, this branch of the famous Tampa restaurant serves paella, chicken Valenciana (baked with yellow rice and smoked ham), red snapper Alicante (a savory seafood casserole), and other Spanish and Cuban specialties.

Le Coq au Vin $$ *4800 South Orange Avenue, Orlando, tel: (407) 851 6980.* Informal, genuinely French country cooking, bistro-style. One of Orlando's best restaurants; frequented by many area chefs.

Dux $$$ *Peabody Hotel, 9801 International Drive, Orlando, tel: (407) 345 4550.* Elegant restaurant serving innovative Northern American cuisine. No duck on the menu, respecting the hotel's resident mascots.

Emeril's Orlando $$$ *Universal Studios CityWalk, 5800 Kirkman Road, Orlando, tel: (407) 224 2424.* One of central Florida's finest dining spots, featuring 'study of duck,' oyster stew, and other inventive fare. Reserve your dining date far in advance.

Hard Rock Café $$ *Universal Studios CityWalk, 5800 Kirkman Road, Orlando, tel: (407) 351 7625.* Burgers and sandwiches, fries and shakes, to the sound of non-stop rock records. Entry from street as well as from studios.

Harvey's Bistro $$ *390 North Orlando Avenue, tel: (407) 246 6560.* A little European style goes a long way at this bistro popular with business lunchers and night-time revelers. Even the humble pot roast is transformed into something special.

Hemingways $$–$$$ *Hyatt Regency Grand Cypress Resort, 1 Grand Cypress Boulevard, tel: (407) 239 1234.* Lobster, crab cakes, steaks, and game are just a few of the hearty entrees served at this inviting shrine to Ernest Hemingway and the atmosphere of Key West. The restaurant overlooks the hotel's huge pool.

Latin Quarter $$$ *CityWalk, tel: (407) 224 2800.* Both food and music are spicy at the Latin Quarter, dedicated to the culture and cuisine of 21 Latin American nations. Diners tuck into platters of *milhojas tostones con cangrejo* (fried plantains with crabmeat), *puerco asado* (roasted pork), paella, and other nuevo latino creations. After dinner, an orchestra and dance troupe take the stage.

Little Saigon Restaurant $$ *1106 E. Colonial Drive, Orlando, tel: (407) 423 8539.* Light, traditional Vietnamese fare in Orlando's busy Asian community.

Macaroni Grill $-$$ *5320 West Erlo Bronson Highway (US 192). Kissimmee, tel: (407) 396 6155.* Italian cuisine. Specialties include *scaloppini di pollo*, *saltimbocca*, and rack of lamb.

Ming Court $$$ *9188 International Drive, Orlando, tel: (407) 351 9988.* A fine variety of Chinese food. Specializing in dim sum.

Park Plaza Gardens $$$ *319 South Park Avenue, Winter Park, tel: (407) 645 2475.* Elegant garden courtyard restaurant featuring Sunday brunch and a fine selection of dinner entrees.

Pebbles $$ *12551 SR 535, at Crossroads, Lake Buena Vista, tel: (407) 827 1111.* Ideas from all over the US (California, Key West) have gone into the menu and the decor.

Race Rock $ *8986 International Drive, tel: (407) 248 9876.* Motorsports restaurant full of stock cars, dragsters, and motorcycles. Expect overstuffed sandwiches, burgers, ribs, pasta, and pizza.

Ran-Getsu $$ *8400 International Drive, Orlando, tel: (407) 345 0044.* Elegant setting for fine Japanese *sushi*, *sukiyaki*, and *tempura*.

The Palm $$$ *Hard Rock Hotel, 5800 Universal Boulevard, tel: (407) 503 7256.* Carnivores can slice into slabs of beef at this knock-off of the famous New York steakhouse – a favorite with the meat and martini crowd. Like the original, there are celebrity caricatures on the wall and a whiff of testosterone in the air.

TooJays $ *72400 East Colonial Drive, Orlando, tel: (407) 894 1718.* An Orlando institution, this is a Jewish deli, diner and home-cooking restaurant. Great sandwiches, main courses, and desserts.

INDEX

Universal Orlando

Vineland Road

UNIVERSAL STUDIOS
FLORIDA

Portofino
Bay Hotel

World
Expo

Major Boulevard

Woody
Woodpecker's
Kidzone

Hard Rock
Hotel

Hollywood

New
York

P

Production
Central

CITYWALK

P

Turkey Lake Road

The
Lost
Continent

Seuss
Landing

Universal Boulevard

Kirkman Road

ISLANDS OF
ADVENTURE

Jurassic
Park

Marvel Super
Hero Island

Toon
Lagoon

Hollywood Way

4

4

← SeaWorld, Discovery Cove

Berlitz® POCKET GUIDE

Walt Disney World® Resort & Orlando

Packed with all the information you need to get the most from your visit

- All the Walt Disney World® Resort parks: Magic Kingdom, Epcot, Disney-MGM Studios, Disney's Animal Kingdom, and Water Parks

- Attractions beyond Disney borders: Universal Studios, Islands of Adventure and CityWalk; SeaWorld Orlando and Wet'n Wild

- Downtown Orlando: Orlando Museum of Art, and Orlando Science Center; plus excursions to Cypress Gardens, Busch Gardens, and the Space Coast

- Restaurant recommendations and lodging options, from modest motels and full-service hotels to lavish Disney-owned resorts

www.berlitzpublishing.com

£4.99

ISBN 981-246-090-X

00499

9 789812 460905

Also from Berli